A HOUSE FOR LIFE

BRINGING THE SPIRIT OF
FRANK LLOYD WRIGHT INTO YOUR HOME

A House for Life: Bringing the Spirit of Frank Lloyd Wright into Your Home
Copyright ©2006 by John Rattenbury

We acknowledge the financial support of the Government of Canada through the Book Publishing Industry Development Program for our publishing activities.

ISBN: 1-894622-40-5

Published by Warwick Publishing Inc.
161 Frederick Street, Suite 200
Toronto, Ontario M5A 4P3 Canada
www.warwickgp.com

Distributed in Canada by
Canadian Book Network
c/o Georgetown Terminal Warehouses
34 Armstrong Avenue
Georgetown, Ontario L7G 4R9
www.canadianbooknetwork.com

Distributed in the United States by
CDS
193 Edwards Drive
Jackson TN 38301
www.cdsbooks.com

Editor: Melinda Tate
Design: Kimberley Young
Copy-Editor: Leo B
Printed in China

Photo page 1: *A house in love with its environment.*
Photo page 2–3: *Simplicity and repose are consequences of harmony.*

A HOUSE FOR LIFE

BRINGING THE SPIRIT OF
FRANK LLOYD WRIGHT INTO YOUR HOME

JOHN RATTENBURY

W

Warwick Publishing
www.warwickgp.com

CONTENTS

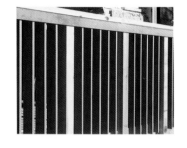

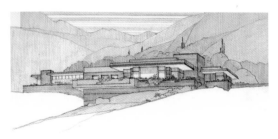

ACKNOWLEDGEMENTS

I had two remarkable teachers in my life — Frank and Olgivanna Lloyd Wright. Both are my heroes. Mr. Wright has been gone since 1959, Mrs. Wright since 1985, yet their presence is as strong as ever. Such remarkable people never die. They live on through their work, their spirit and their ideas.

Many thanks to my colleagues at Taliesin — the members of our architectural firm, our school and our community. Writing this book required considerable research and I was fortunate to have the resources of the William Wesley Peters Library at Taliesin West. Our librarians, Elizabeth Dawsari and Helen Hynes, together with Dennis Madden, our archivist, were able to find answers to my questions, no matter how strange or obscure.

Bruce Pfeiffer, director of the Frank Lloyd Wright Archives, reviewed my text on Frank Lloyd Wright's ideas for moderate-cost houses, and his colleague Oskar Munoz photographed many drawings of my projects.

Nothing escaped the eagle eye of my sister-in-law, Tari Wood. She patiently and methodically read the manuscript and made many useful suggestions. My sincere thanks to Gerry Jones, Charlie Main and family, Jack Skinner, Tom Casey and Ryc Loope. They also took the trouble to offer constructive criticism. My colleague, Gustad Irani, filled in for me in the studio while I spent time writing.

The houses for Sandy Sims, Robert West and Wayne McBroom are Frank Lloyd Wright designs that I adapted to new sites. All the other projects illustrated in this book are my designs. I drew most of the renderings with colored pencils.

I have had a difficult time crediting the photography because the work extends back so long in time. Some of the photographers are:

Michael French (Theilen, Sims, Myers)

Anthony Peres (Myers)

Wayne Sorce (Life House at Gold Mountain)

Arthur Coleman and Daniel Ruark (Sunsprite & Sunstream)

Ed Obma and Pedro Guerrero (FLLW, OLLW, Taliesin Fellowship)

Layne Kennedy (Canoe Bay)

Frank Zullo (Desert Mountain).

I shot many of the photographs myself, some of them over the shoulder of a professional photographer. These talented people often let me take interior shots after they had set up the lighting and even suggested the best type of lens, speed and aperture settings. Their generosity gave me an education in photography. My apologies to photographers who are not credited.

I will forever be grateful to my first client, Dan Kessler. He gave me free rein in designing the house for his family in New Jersey. The summer that I worked on his house, the Fellowship had a temporary office in Europe. This was Mrs. Wright's way to broaden our education. Dan and his wife Helene came to Switzerland to see the drawings, telling his friends that he had to go a long way to see his architect. Mrs. Wright gave me advice on color schemes, as she had done for Mr. Wright.

In 1967 Dan was kind enough to pay my way to Japan. Several of us went to Tokyo with Mrs. Wright to try to save the Imperial Hotel from being torn down. Dan also gave me money to buy art objects for his house. In Kyoto I purchased a collection of Japanese screens and antiques that were later appraised at five times their purchase price. The pieces that he didn't use he let me keep.

I have had the good fortune to be blessed with many wonderful clients who trusted and believed in me. Most of them became lifelong friends.

In 1996 my wife Kay left this earth to join Mr. and Mrs. Wright. She was my best friend and partner in life, architecture and education for forty-six years. We worked together in architecture, she as the interior designer. This book is dedicated to her.

The front door sets the theme.

INTRODUCTION

Any building for humane purposes should be an elemental, sympathetic feature of the ground, complementary to its natural environment, belonging by kinship to the terrain.

— Frank Lloyd Wright

I t is my belief that Frank Lloyd Wright's timeless ideas for designing and building a beautiful and functional home should be accessible to everybody. Over forty years since he left us, his philosophy is as relevant as ever and his ideas continue to find an ever-increasing audience.

In 1954 he wrote *The Natural House,* which was published by Ben Raeburn of Horizon Press. It set forth, in simple and comprehensible terms, his ideas for a house of modest size and cost. At the time it came out I had served as one of his apprentices for four years. I remember my excitement. It was the first book on residential architecture that struck a chord in my heart. The book was illustrated with many of the homes that Wright created in the forties and fifties. The timeless aspect of their designs is still clear half a century later.

Since the nature of organic architecture is one of constant growth, it seems appropriate to show how the Natural House continues to evolve today. Wright used the term "organic" because he never cared for the word "modern," which implies something in the mode, a design that is in and then out of fashion. For art to transcend time it must have an enduring quality. Because his philosophy of architecture was rooted in Nature, which is itself both timeless and constantly evolving, he chose the word "organic," a term first used by his mentor, the architect Louis Sullivan.

Organic architecture should not be confused with the Art Deco or Art Nouveau styles that were popular in Europe and America in the first part of the twentieth century. Like all "styles," they came and went. Styles are sometimes

Bas-relief design in stained wood and copper for a front door.

The concept of open space is the liberation of architecture.

dusted off, revived for a while, only to fade back again into history. Although Wright was sometimes listed among architects who were proponents of Art Deco, his work clearly transcends all styles and fashions.

Around the turn of the century he began to refer to the houses he was designing for the Midwest as "Prairie Houses." Later he called them "Usonian," a word coined by Samuel Butler to distinguish the United States from the rest of the Americas. Eventually Wright settled on the word "organic" to describe his architecture.

Most architects start their careers by designing houses, but are eager for the opportunity to design larger buildings. When they get bigger commissions they usually give up designing houses, which they believe bring small compensation for the amount of work involved. Frank Lloyd Wright was extraordinary because he continued to design houses all his life. He received commissions for many large projects, such as the Imperial Hotel in Tokyo, Japan, and the Guggenheim Museum in New York, yet his interest in houses never waned. A few of his homes were for wealthy clients, but most were for families of moderate means. He paid as much attention to a small house as he did to a large building.

What do I consider to be the essence of Wright's legacy? Even more significant than the beautiful structures he designed are the lessons that he taught us. I believe we should try to understand the principles on which these designs are based. While a principle itself is a simple, fundamental truth — so broad as to be immutable — it can, and should, be expressed by an infinite variety of forms. There can be no absolute in the application of a principle. When we apply the absolute to its expression, we kill the very thing that the principle upholds. Because the concept of organic architecture is based on principles, it will not only endure but also constantly evolve into new and appropriate forms.

The greatest example of principles at work in design is to be found in Nature. The design of everything in the cosmos, from the structure of the atom to the configuration of the universe, follows fundamental principles. They underlie the structure, appearance and function of all plants and animals as well as all inanimate matter.

A pine tree, for example, demonstrates the same general design principles as a maple tree. Each has a structural system of roots that anchors it to the earth and resists the force of the wind. Each has a trunk that rises up into the sky and branches that extend into the sunlight. Although the leaves of these trees are quite unalike, they both have a similar purpose — to absorb solar energy. Both trees use their roots to collect nourishment from the soil; both use the process of photosynthesis to manufacture food with sunlight. Both reproduce using seeds. Yet, while following the same principles of design, the appearance of the pine is totally different from the maple — in size, form, color and texture. Each is functional and beautiful in its own distinct way.

Herein lies the secret of organic architecture. When we follow the fundamental and

A home should be practical, beautiful and inspiring.

The "Natural House" continues to evolve.

unchanging principles of Nature we have the opportunity to create an unending variety of forms and shapes. Just as the creations of nature are timeless, disciplined in their design yet infinite in their variety of form, so are the structures of organic architecture.

In my book, *A Living Architecture,* I described Wright's twelve architectural principles:

1. Inspiration and Ideas
2. Integrity and Unity
3. Humanity and Spirit
4. Harmony with the Environment
5. Space, Form & the Third Dimension
6. Structural Continuity
7. The Nature of Materials
8. Character
9. Beauty and Romance
10. Simplicity and Repose
11. Decentralization
12. Freedom

My purpose in writing this book is to pass on what I have learned, in philosophic and practical terms, about what makes a home practical, beautiful and inspiring.

Yesterday is history, tomorrow is a mystery, but today is a gift.

—Alicia Bristow

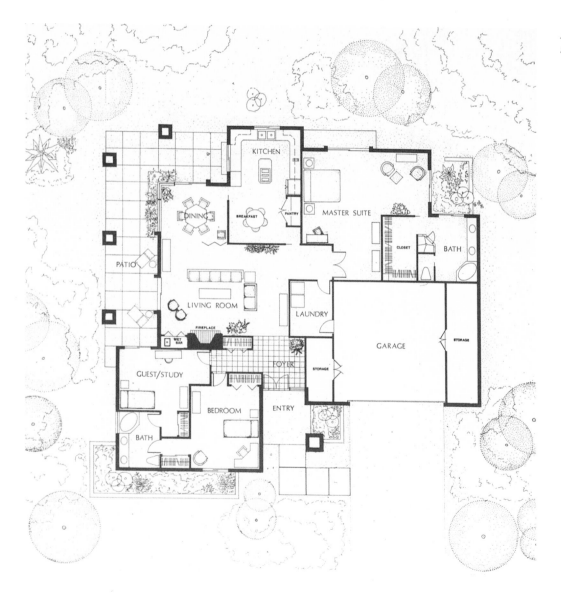

A small but spacious three-bedroom house.

FINDING TALIESIN

*If a man does not keep pace with his company, perhaps it is because he hears a different drummer.
Let him step to the music he hears, however measured or far away.*

—Henry David Thoreau

How is it that I came to Taliesin early in my life and why have I stayed here ever since? What is the source of my passion for architecture and education?

It goes back to my childhood. When I was barely a teenager, I instinctively felt that in return for the gift of life on this earth I should strive to give something back — some bit of wisdom inherited from my parents, my teachers, or some past life, no doubt. As I grew up, this feeling started to evolve from instinct into a conscious recognition.

I certainly made many mistakes, but all those life experiences, good and bad, were opportunities to learn. As I matured I began to sense the quiet sound of an intriguing inner voice. Gradually I became aware it was telling me that I should search for some meaning to life. At this point I had embarked on a fascinating quest, one that would last a lifetime.

As I look back on the years past, I can appreciate the circumstances and coincidences that have shaped my life.

My father, Frances Mawson Rattenbury, born in 1867, was a prominent Canadian architect. At the age of twenty-five he designed British Columbia's Parliament Buildings in Victoria. Commissions for the Empress Hotel and the Crystal Gardens followed. My mother, Alma Victoria Clarke, was a concert pianist and composer. We lived in a house designed by my father on the oceanfront of Oak Bay, a suburb of Victoria. I had an older brother, Christopher, who became a commercial artist.

When I was two, our family set sail for England, where we settled in Bournemouth. Father resumed his architectural practice, on a smaller scale, and Mother wrote music. My memory

Iechinehal — the Rattenbury home in Victoria, British Columbia.

Top: *The Empress Hotel, Victoria, British Columbia — designed by my father.*

Above: *The British Columbia Parliament Buildings — also designed by my father.*

of my parents is sketchy, but when I was four I experienced something I have never forgotten. Mother was playing the grand piano in the living room. Hearing the music, I came in from the garden where I had been industriously digging up her flowers.

Near the piano was an easel, low to the ground, with a drawing of a building that Father had designed: clean, straight lines drawn on crisp white paper. An entrance door and steps. Trees on either side. Some hand lettering. The beautiful image was etched so sharply in my mind that I can recall it clearly to this day.

At that moment I started a love affair with the beauty of pencil lines on paper.

My parents both died when I was five. For the next six years I went to English boarding schools, ending up at King's College Choir School in Cambridge. In 1939, England declared war on Germany and the Axis powers. A Nazi invasion seemed imminent, so in the summer of 1941 I was sent to Canada to live with my grandmother and brother in Vancouver. Here I attended a private school, St. George's, and enjoyed the benefits of small classes and good teachers.

It was here that I had my first taste of architecture. Since the school was getting old and worn out, the headmaster proposed a student competition to design a new campus. He offered a prize to the winner. I submitted a sketch. The main focus of my design was a large assembly room/gymnasium, which featured a floor that slid back to reveal a swimming pool

underneath. The teachers (to whom we referred as "masters") were confined to a small and remote building. Everything in the school was devoted to the comfort of the students. The most luxurious room was the infirmary, where students could lie in bed and look down through a window into the gymnasium and pool below. Despite its complete impracticality, the concept won first prize (probably because only two other students entered and neither completed their drawings). When I received the award of five dollars, my fate was sealed: I must become an architect. It was fun and it was rewarding.

Eventually I enrolled at the University of British Columbia, but before I could enter the School of Architecture I had to take one year of liberal arts and two years of engineering. I struggled through French, Psychology, Chemistry, Physics and Calculus, unable to see what they had to do with architecture. Evenings were spent solving endless structural equations. As I struggled to calculate the trusses for a theoretical steel bridge, I wondered when I would get to design buildings.

After two years, having run through my inheritance, I went to work for a logging company in northern British Columbia. Here I learned to operate a bulldozer and fire a steam locomotive, accomplishments that gave me some self-confidence. I worked long hours and earned

Taliesin West — a National Historic Landmark.

enough to continue my education, planning on attending a much smaller school. I selected Oregon State College, where a new Department of Architecture had just been established. There were only twenty-five students and two professors. The size was perfect and the teachers were excellent. I began to study in earnest.

One evening I had what might be called a defining moment. I went to the college library to get some research material. By chance, I picked up a book entitled, *In the Nature of Materials,* by Frank Lloyd Wright — a name unknown to me. The moment I opened the cover I was astonished. I had no idea that architecture could be so beautiful, so exciting, so different. The designs were quite unlike the old classical forms that my father embraced, or the cold and severe shapes of modern architecture that were becoming popular and being promoted in architectural schools.

Mr. Wright critiques my design for a Box project.

Wright referred to his architecture as "organic," and his ideas made a good deal of sense. He expressed an underlying philosophy that connected architecture to Nature. This was something I could fully appreciate. I was so intrigued that I stayed up all night reading. I learned that Wright's home was called Taliesin.

In the summer I returned to Vancouver and got a job with William Frederick Gardiner, a semi-retired architect. He already had two young employees in the office, Larry Bruin and Jackson Wong. A kind man, he only took me on because he had known my father. At a salary of fifty dollars a week I was getting my first experience in architecture.

It turned out that both Larry and Jackson were

great admirers of Wright. They had a copy of the 1948 *Architectural Forum* with wonderful illustrations of his recent designs. Furthermore, they had discovered that there was a group of apprentices called the Taliesin Fellowship, and Jackson was planning to join them. Applicants had to send $200 in advance and have a personal interview with Mr. Wright.

In the summer of 1950 I made a decision. Larry was driving to Detroit, and was dropping Jackson off along the way at Taliesin in Wisconsin. Acting on blind faith that I would be accepted by the Fellowship, I packed a small suitcase and joined them. I would not return to Vancouver for over thirty years.

We crossed into the United States and drove east for several days. As our car neared Taliesin, my anticipation grew. I had yet to see an actual building designed by Wright. In Wisconsin we passed through the little town of Richland Center, just forty miles west of Spring Green. Looking out of the car window I saw a structure that I was sure must be his design. I jumped out and stood on the sidewalk, my mouth agape. The building was just a warehouse but it was beautiful. Red brick walls were topped with a buff-colored concrete frieze sculptured in geometric patterns.

A stylish lady who was passing by saw me staring. She paused, "You must be one of the boys from Taliesin," she said.

"No," I responded, "but that is where I want to go."

"Well," she said, "when you do you will meet my daughter Kay." The lady turned out to be Viva Schneider. She was the daughter of A. D. German, the client for whom Mr. Wright had designed the building in 1915. She was Kay's stepmother.

As we drove up the hill to Taliesin I felt like I was in a dream. I had never experienced anything so beautiful. Asked to wait outside until Mr. Wright appeared, we wandered up to the crest of the hill around which Taliesin is wrapped.

The feeling I had was one of "coming home." The buildings and landscape seemed to grow out of the hill, as though they had been there forever. An enormous oak tree spread out its green canopy above us. The gardens were filled with color — scarlet cardinal flowers, magenta phlox, orange day lilies, pink and ivory hollyhocks. The rough texture of golden-buff limestone walls and chimneys contrasted with sand-colored stucco. The window sash was painted a rust-red color. Gently sloping cedar-shingle roofs extended into space and created deep shadows.

It was a poem, a world of magic. It had a spiritual quality that moved me deeply. As I sat there in the

Mrs. Wright. It was her idea to start a school of architecture.

Bottom: *Mr. Wright "edits" Kay's sculpture.*

My first attempt at sculpture — a fountain for Mrs. Wright.

garden waiting, a door below opened. Two women stepped out, one wearing a soft, white gown and wide-brimmed summer hat. Her beauty and graceful movements struck me forcibly. I didn't know it then, but this was Mr. Wright's wife, Olgivanna. The attractive person beside her, I found out later, was Kay. These two people were to change my life.

As I entered the building I felt that the space was so enchanting it transcended time. I never imagined that architecture could be so beautiful. The air was permeated with the mixed fragrance of cypress boards and bouquets of wild antimony.

My first impression of Mr. Wright was of his magnetic presence. If his architecture was spellbinding, so was he. He was eighty-two at the time, sixty-one years older than I, but he clearly had the quality of youth. He spent a few minutes with me, asked only a few questions, but I felt that he saw into my soul. Rather than directly telling me whether or not I was accepted as an apprentice, he said, "We are about to head to Arizona. We'll see you there." On this enigmatic note he walked out of his office, leaving us in a quandary. Jackson was all for going back to Vancouver but I insisted we find our way south.

Larry was going on to Detroit so we continued heading east. Passing through Chicago, we heard about a job opportunity. Automobile dealers in Phoenix needed people to deliver cars from the factory in Detroit. They paid drivers fifty dollars to cover fuel expenses and allowed

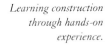

Learning construction through hands-on experience.

them five days for the trip. Jackson and I picked up a brand new Ford sedan at the factory and crossed the U.S. In three days we arrived in Phoenix.

Since the Fellowship had not yet arrived at Taliesin West we got temporary jobs and waited. After several weeks we heard they were back and an interview was scheduled. We waited in the reception office and when Mr. Wright came in, his secretary, Gene Masselink, introduced us. He recognized us immediately as the two Canadians from Vancouver.

I suppose I was expecting him to ask us questions about our education. Instead he entertained us with a brief story, then got up and walked out. As he left, he said, "See Nils about tents." What did that mean? Gene kindly explained that we had been accepted; we should find Nils Schweizer, the apprentice who distributed the tents.

As it turned out no tents were available, so we spent several nights sleeping under the stars. I was so excited I could hardly close my eyes anyway.

That winter was spent on construction work, painting, pouring concrete, taking turns as "kitchen helper." Soon I was immersed in a wide variety of activities: construction, farming, gardening, washing dishes, sweeping floors — all the tasks necessary to sustain Fellowship life. This was nothing remotely like other architectural schools, where students spent all day in class and the evenings in study. This was about experiential learning. Every moment was full of activity. I was eager to rise in the morning and sorry to have to go to bed.

Providence has played a significant role in my life. How else can I explain finding mentors and spiritual parents to replace the ones that I lost when I was five. Or the coincidences — my father's name was Frank, he was an architect and he was born in 1867, the same year as Frank Lloyd Wright. My mother was a concert pianist and composer, a generation younger than my father. Olgivanna was some thirty years younger than her husband and she composed music; we even have the same birth date, December 27. The year that I was born, Frank and Olgivanna were married in Rancho Santa Fe, California.

Mr. Wright drew every design with a simple wood pencil.

THE TALIESIN FELLOWSHIP

What a society honors will be cultivated

— Aristotle

When I arrived at Taliesin in 1950 I was twenty-one, with energy to burn. Yet I never was able to keep up with Mr. Wright. Both his stamina and his creative abilities were extraordinary. He generated so many new ideas that they seemed to pour out of him, literally spilling out onto paper. Like the magician Merlin, he seemed to shake designs out of his sleeve.

There were fifty apprentices in the Taliesin Fellowship, an amalgamation of different colors and creeds, a mixture of ages and nationalities, young boys and girls who came from all over the world. The only distinction made was that those who had served for several years and arrived at a position of trust and loyalty were designated as senior apprentices. They received a monthly stipend and had a small car. We all worked together at every kind of job.

Continuing a tradition that started in 1932 when the Taliesin Fellowship was founded, the senior apprentices supervised the newer ones in their work. They

The studio at Taliesin West — headquarters of Taliesin Architects.

Teamwork.

Below: *Constructing the Pavilion at Taliesin West.*

served as a conduit for learning from Mr. Wright. Although these seniors were still called apprentices, they were in actuality his associates and were given considerable responsibility and authority. All were talented architects and artists, dedicated to Taliesin.

Mr. Wright watched over all the work in the studio, construction and the farm; social activities, cooking and resolution of any personal problems he left to Mrs. Wright.

There are two campuses. In the fall the Fellowship travels south to Taliesin West in Arizona. In the spring, most of the group travels north to Taliesin in Wisconsin. We often make the trip in a caravan of cars, camping out along the way. This is a great chance to see America, another learning opportunity.

All people who are involved in a creative act seek some form of inspiration. This doesn't just apply to architects,

artists, actors, writers and musicians; it applies to entrepreneurs, scientists, doctors and educators; to farmers, cooks, builders, business people and politicians. We are all creating something and we all need to be inspired.

At Taliesin we seek ways to nourish the creative spirit. Our community, which we call the Taliesin Fellowship, includes people from all over the world. We participate in social and cultural events — music, art, poetry and drama. We ask visiting lecturers to share their ideas with us. We constantly explore ways to escape traditional thinking. Our aim is get ourselves out of a rut, to break the habitual patterns of a lifetime that bind us like ropes.

Frank Lloyd Wright made it clear that he wanted his work to be emulated, not imitated. *Emulation* means striving to equal or exceed, as opposed to *imitation*, which means copying or mimicking. At the center of the continuing exploration of organic architecture is a group of architects who worked with Wright. Our efforts are dedicated to the discovery of new ways to spread timeless ideas. We share a common mission — to inspire future generations to strive to exceed the work of the past.

While Mr. Wright was alive he was in our midst every day, inspiring and encouraging us. He constantly amazed us with fresh ideas, delighted us with his sense of humor, and astonished us with his creative energy.

After I had spent a year at Taliesin, working on construction and the farm, I was given a chance to work in the studio. Mr. Wright had a desk at one end, but he liked to roam around and stop at apprentices' desks.

"Move over, John," he would say, "let's see what you have here." I would slide to the side of the sheepskin-covered bench and he would sit down next to me at my drafting board, thoughtfully studying the drawing on which I was working. The first time it was a small seaside cottage for George Clark in Carmel, California. I had taken Wright's rough sketch and drawn the floor plan and elevations. After a moment, his sharp eye caught something. He picked up my pencil and in a few swift, sure strokes, he adjusted the roofline. Then he was up, out the door and off to check on how the construction of a new stone wall was coming along. A whirlwind of action, he accomplished it all with grace rather than haste.

After I had been at Taliesin for some years I fell in love with a fellow apprentice. Kay Schneider was one of the first to join the Taliesin Fellowship and at the age of fifteen she was certainly the youngest. Kay loved to draw and when she was growing up she had had a small desk next to her father's.

Heinrich Schneider was Swiss, and a brilliant engineer and inventor. Amongst his numerous

Top: *Apprentices presenting designs for a critique.*

Middle: *The Taliesin ensemble.*

Bottom: *The Taliesin chorus.*

inventions was the hydromatic drive for automobiles. This was the precursor to today's automatic shift.

After World War I, the family moved from Switzerland to Beloit, Wisconsin, just 150 miles from Taliesin. Mr. Schneider knew and admired Frank Lloyd Wright and took Kay to meet him when she was fourteen. That meeting defined her destiny, and she determined to become an architect. Although she was very young, her father was willing to entrust Mr. and Mrs. Wright with his daughter's education. So she left home and came to live and work at Taliesin. She drove a car that was unlike anything else on the road. It had the first working model of her father's automatic gearshift.

At Taliesin, Kay continued to develop her skills. She was already accomplished at both drawing and painting (portraits and landscapes). Now she learned architecture and interior design. Soon we were working as colleagues. Over the years we worked on many projects across the country and overseas. Although officially I was the architect and she was the interior designer, we blurred the roles. She helped me with the architecture and I enjoyed assisting her with interior designs.

Among Kay's many abilities was a natural skill to organize. Soon after she arrived at Taliesin she was put in charge of the "worklist," the weekly assignments of members of the Fellowship to kitchen duties and maintenance tasks.

Whereas most of the apprentices flocked around Mr. Wright, Kay recognized the role that Mrs. Wright played. She began to help her by typing letters and answering phone calls. Before long she became her trusted associate.

After she had been at Taliesin for a few years, Kay was put in charge of the kitchen. When Mrs. Wright discovered that she had a natural aptitude, she taught her to cook. Together they began to collect recipes from all over the world and created *The Taliesin Cookbook*.

Kay handled her managerial role with both objectivity and tact. Although small in size (I used to tease her that she never weighed as much as a sack of Portland cement) she was totally fearless. She often had to go to battle with Mr. Wright's son-in-law, William Wesley Peters.

Wes was both an architect and engineer and did the structural design for many of Mr. Wright's buildings. He was also in charge of construction work at Taliesin and Taliesin West and supervised a crew of apprentices who worked hard to keep up with Mr. Wright's building program.

Though Wes was a big man — six foot four inches tall — and had a forceful nature, he never won a battle with Kay. Wes always needed more manpower to get the work done. But when the time came for an apprentice to go on kitchen duty, Kay stood her ground. All Wes could do was clench his hands together and grind his teeth.

As one of the first women at Taliesin, Kay did not have an easy time. The male apprentices tended to think that architects should be men. Howev er, they soon found out that neither Mr. or Mrs. Wright believed this. On the contrary, they felt that the practice of democracy in our life and work at Taliesin would afford us special opportunities to learn about the many cultures of the world. Today we have an equal number of male and female apprentices at the Frank Lloyd Wright School of Architecture, many of them from outside the United States.

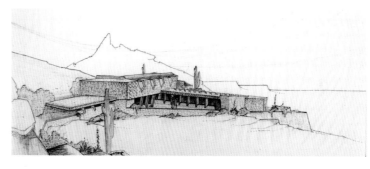

Top: *Sketch I made of Mr. Wright's house for Marilyn Monroe.*

Middle and bottom: *A house I designed for "The Box." Mr. Wright's critiques were invaluable.*

WHY WE BUILD

What is architecture? It is man and more. It is man in possession of his earth. It is the only true record of him where his possession of the earth is concerned.

—FLLW

We must all, at some time, dream of living in a beautiful house. These dreams usually start in our early childhood, when we pile up cardboard boxes, heap pillows together and hang up sheets. We are creating a cozy space into which we can crawl. A set of building blocks, a toy construction kit, a dollhouse — all are excellent learning tools. If there are trees nearby, there will be an opportunity to build a treehouse. Our basic instincts are leading us to this primal idea of creating a home of our own.

Home building is a natural, hereditary instinct for many living creatures. Some build nests, others dig holes in the ground. Some, such as snails, carry their home around with them. As humans evolved, so did awareness of the need to create better shelter from the weather and protection from predators. Their first home was a cave. Then came simple structures of wood, mud, stones or bricks. Roofs were branches and plant leaves or animal skins. The first roof tiles were large flat stones.

The progress of a civilization can be followed by the way its architectural structures and forms evolved. Most of the earliest structures were both simple and beautiful, often because the limitations of technology meant the builders had to respect the basic nature of the materials with which they built.

Opposite: *Organic architecture is an integral part of the landscape.*

Below: Of *the hill and not* on *the hill.*

The curved forms of walls and domes complement Nature.

Opposite: *Unity means every part belongs and is in harmony.*

Evidence of this simplicity and beauty can be found in many structures around the world. We see examples in Native American pueblos and wigwams, Egyptian and Mayan pyramids, Islamic mosques, Gothic cathedrals, Oriental temples and pagodas, and the native huts in Africa. These all fit the description of a natural, organic architecture. The Potala at Lhasa in Tibet is a great example of organic design.

If we had beautiful architecture in ancient times, what happened to it in the colonizing of America? A witty Frenchman said, "America is the only country to have proceeded directly from barbarism to degeneracy with no culture of its own in between."

If the progress of a civilization can largely be judged by the quality of its art and architecture, how will people in the third millennium regard us? What contemporary architecture do we have that will stand the test of time? We do have some notable buildings and structures, but what about the houses we live in? What percentage of the homes in America do you believe represent good architecture?

Why do we build a house? The simplest answer is, to provide shelter from the elements. If this is so, then shouldn't our house express a sense of shelter in its design? We build houses to accommodate the various activities of life — living, cooking, dining, entertaining, sleeping, bathing and storing our "stuff." So shouldn't the plan of our home be based on these functions and their interrelationships? Our house is an opportunity to create an environment that will make all these activities flow smoothly. But it should do much more than just be

functional. It should nurture the family and sustain its spirit. To do these things, a house should be beautiful. It should add to, not detract from, the natural beauty of the landscape.

A primary objective for many people in the world today, especially in America, is the accumulation of wealth. Our house often becomes a way to show off to others how successful we are in becoming rich. For those who can afford it, this may be an understandable, though somewhat crude reason. But for the family with a moderate income, it means spending a part of the budget just to impress the neighbors. I believe our resources are better invested in nurturing our family.

In any event, real wealth in life tends to be intangible. Money helps, but some things are not for sale — love and appreciation of one's family, friendship, good health, a sense of joy, and a faith in the possibility of earning immortality.

Beauty is a quality that enriches life immeasurably, one that can and should be pursued by everybody. The sort of beauty that is universal and timeless we can call *objective,* as opposed to *subjective.* What is the difference? Subjective beauty is an opinion of the beholder, whereas objective beauty is something almost everybody can agree upon. We see it in Nature. There is universal agreement on the beauty of a sunrise, snow-capped mountains, lakes, trees and flowers. Most of the creatures of this earth are beautiful. When you see a mother's love for her child, this is a part of Nature, and surely its beauty is objective. From the formation of the stars and planets — the macrocosm — down to the structure of the atom — the microcosm, everything in creation is full of examples of objective beauty.

Some things created by humanity have also achieved objective beauty. This does not mean that every person will see them as beautiful, but a vast majority of people, regardless of who they are or where they come from, will see this quality. It may be a piece of music, a painting, some sculpture or a poem — their beauty is something beyond the eye of the beholder. Beauty touches our spirit. It has magical powers to uplift and enlighten us.

If beauty is something to be sought after, should it not be an essential feature of the home in which we live? Our man-made environment affects us every minute that we are in it. If our home is beautiful, it will make us feel better from the moment we wake up. It will inspire us and lift our spirits when we are depressed, energize us, and help us to relax when we are tired. It can add so much to our lives.

This is the goal of organic architecture — a goal that is always exploring, ever expanding, unending. It aims to put mankind in harmony with our natural heritage, with our planet Earth.

Every genuine work of art has as much reason for being as the earth and the sun.
                                                            —Ralph Waldo Emerson

Architecture is man in possession of his earth.

BEDROOM

BEDROOM

DRESS

LAUNDRY

DRESS

W O

MSTR BEDROOM

MECH

DN

C.

ST

BAR

STUDY

DN

SUN ROOM

ENTRY

POOL

LAWN

DN

UP

COVE

F.P.

CT

TV

PANTRY STOR

DINING

KITCHEN

BREAKFAST

LIVING ROOM

DINING TERRACE

A sense of free space starts with an open plan.

DESTROYING THE BOX

What a society honors will be cultivated.

—Aristotle

It is time for the American house to come out of the dark ages and into the future. The most cherished quality that we have in America is freedom. It is the essence of our democracy. Millions of people have died fighting to preserve it, and we hope that one day everybody in the world will share in it.

Traditional values mean more than traditional forms.

VIEW FROM SOUTHEAST

Furnishings designed as a part of the architecture.

Why shouldn't this precious idea of democracy extend to architecture? A home that represents the spirit of freedom will have free and open space. It will not be just a box, a container for people.

The traditional post and beam method of construction, which we inherited from the ancient Greeks, puts vertical supports at each corner and then fills in the space with walls or columns. The point where the walls meet the roof is another corner, but in this case a horizontal corner rather than a vertical one. To let in daylight, holes are cut in the outer walls to create windows. The form is just a box — a square, a rectangle, or any other shape. It may be ornamented, it may be surrounded by columns, it may have all sorts of features applied to it, but it is still a box.

Why do most houses still follow box-like shapes? I attribute it to passivity and a lack of imagination on the part of designers and builders. With the construction technology and variety of materials available, we have the means to liberate architectural space. Narrow lots also force houses into rectilinear shapes.

Since a box is defined by its vertical corners and its horizontal edges, the first thing we can do is to eliminate the corner post. Now the corner may be left open or perhaps replaced with glass. As the corner is opened up, the box begins to disappear.

To remove the edge of the box, the roof is extended out from the enclosing walls. The roof now becomes a broad and protective brow that provides shelter and shade. The walls are just screens in space. Some can be transparent or translucent. The floor plan becomes an open-space plan, with one space flowing naturally into another space.

Geometry. I base my designs on a modular system derived from three basic geometric shapes — the square, the triangle, the circle — and combinations of these configurations. These key two-dimensional shapes, when most simply expressed in the third dimension, become the cube, the pyramid, the cylinder and the sphere.

Yet despite the simplicity of basing designs on such uncomplicated fundamental shapes, there are countless ways

Above: Curved forms are sympathetic to the human shape.

We have the means to liberate architecture.

Transforming space and transcending time.

Below: *Interior space determines exterior form.*

to manifest them as architecture. There is no limitation to the forms and shapes that come with a little imagination.

To the square and rectangle are added the octagon, the cruciform and ell-shape. The triangle, diamond and hexagon give rise to totally different designs. A form that should be given more consideration for a house is the circle. The circle is efficient — it encloses more space for a given length of wall than a square or rectangle. It is a more human shape. Our body is all curves; it has no right angles, so we feel more comfortable in a round shape. The circle is the symbol of infinity and a circular room will seem more spacious. The circle can also be facetted, or broken up into many straight pieces. This method will accommodate flat windows and doors (which are impractical to curve). In Nature, almost everything is curved, from the planets in their orbits to the clouds, the trees and the molecular structure of everything we perceive.

Some materials are easily laid up in curves — masonry units, concrete, tile, plaster and EIFS (exterior insulation finish system). If the radius is not too tight, drywall can be curved. Wood and metal studs are easily set to form curved walls. Sometimes it serves just to have a few curved walls in your home. In the 1997 Life Dream House there are three curved spaces — the dining area, the study and a part of the master bedroom.

Out of clutter, find simplicity.
From discord, find harmony.
In the middle of difficulty lies opportunity.

—Albert Einstein

WORKING WITH AN ARCHITECT

No man can build a building for another who does not believe in him, who does not believe in what he believes in, and who has not chosen him because of this faith, knowing what he can do. That is the nature of architect and client.

—FLLW

Let's ask the question: Who is the best person to design your home? I believe it is you. You and your family. After all, you are the ones who are going to live in it. So why do you need an architect? Because an architect has a special combination of artistic, scientific and business skills and experience.

The best service your architect can provide is to design a house that is *just for you.* Remember that an architect is only doing for you *what you would do yourself,* if you had the ability. Architects should never be allowed to build monuments to themselves.

CAN YOU AFFORD AN ARCHITECT?

The perception of many people is that they cannot afford an architect for a moderate-cost home. This may come from not clearly understanding what we do, so let's talk about it. I would like to persuade you that a good architect could save you so much, you cannot afford to proceed without one.

To start with, we systematically determine just what you want in your new house. This is a big investment you are making, one you should make with great care. Are you clear on the basic goals for your new home? What should it do for you?

Your architect should ensure that your fundamental objectives are achieved. Then you get down to the specifics — what type of spaces, how large, and so on. The long-term payback will be a beautiful and functional home that provides your family with many years of enjoyment and fulfillment. Your home will not only contribute to your quality of life for many

Opposite: *Working with apprentices — learning by doing.*

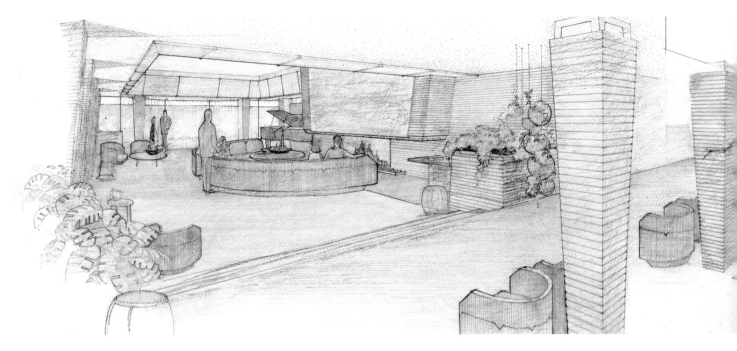

Presentation rendering made with colored pencils.

years, but will have an excellent chance of yielding a high return on investment if the time comes to sell.

What should you expect architects to charge for their services? There is no standard fee in the profession. Our firm's normal charge is fifteen percent of the construction cost, which is defined as the cost of everything that we design or specify.

Our services generally include programming, site planning, conceptual design, preliminary cost estimating, design development, landscape design, interior design, construction documents, guidance in selecting a builder, assistance during the bidding or negotiating phase, and observation of the construction. Once the scope of work and budget have been confirmed, we are willing to convert our fee to a lump sum.

I expect to work within a budget. My success as an architect is in no small way related to my concern that there be no cost overruns or surprises.

THE BEST WAY TO SELECT AN ARCHITECT

An architect, when asked for references, should tell you to call anybody they have ever worked for, not just hand you a carefully selected list. Go to see his or her work. Pictures are useful, but if possible, get inside a house that the architect has designed and meet the clients. Ask them about their experience. Then talk to contractors who have built a home designed by the architect you are considering.

Take as much care selecting your architect as you would in selecting your doctor. Remember that you are determining the shape and quality of an environment that will affect you and your family for years to come.

What should you expect of your architect? First of all, good service. Your architect should take the time to get to know you and the key members of your family. This means spending time together and asking lots of questions. It means paying a visit to your site, or if this is not feasible, carefully studying a topographic map and photographs.

Probably one of the biggest mistakes people make is to plunge into the design of a house before they have clearly defined their needs. This results in a "hit and miss" approach to creating a floor plan. The initial part of any design procedure should be what architects call "programming."

PROGRAMMING YOUR REQUIREMENTS

"A problem well stated is a problem half solved," said Charles Kettering, so this is the process architects use to determine, quantify and prioritize a client's needs — types of activities and spaces needed, their sizes and interrelationships. Programming is a way to understand a problem, as opposed to design, which is solving a problem. In order to design an appropriate home, an architect needs to understand how you and your family want to live. After spending time with you to understand your requirements, your architect will develop a list of activities and spaces and assign tentative sizes to the various areas.

However, you may want to start the programming process before you talk to an architect. Since many homeowners are unfamiliar with the process, here is an explanation of how to proceed.

I suggest that you start with a meeting

Apprentice making a model.

Study model to verify relationship to site.

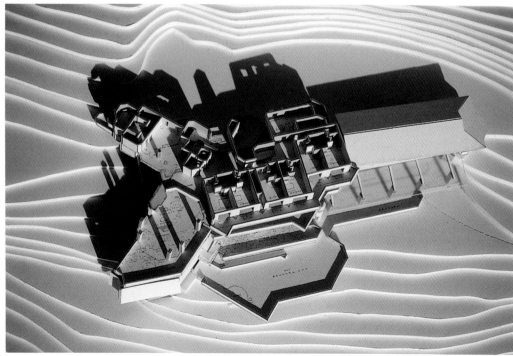

Plan of the 1997 Life Dream House.

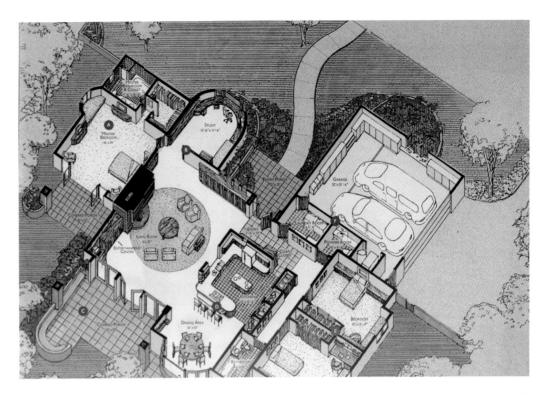

of your family, perhaps on a weekend. Gather around the dining table and give each person a pad of paper. Select one member of the family as the "coordinator." Pass out a list of activities that you have prepared in advance.

The list should include all the basic functions: Entry, Living, Entertainment, Dining, Cooking, Storage, Sleeping, Washing (Parents' quarters and Children's quarters), Recreation, Study, Hobbies, Guests, Parking, Outdoor Activities and so forth. The more that each member of the family is engaged in the process, the more they will feel that it is their home.

Let everybody list their own personal goals, long term and short term, and then try to decide on some priorities. Consider "space adjacencies." Some spaces obviously need to be close together. Bedrooms should be near a bathroom. The kitchen needs to be near the dining area. But some spaces should be separated. Do you want the master bedroom near the children's rooms?

Programming is an essential step in ensuring that your new home will serve you effectively. At this point, cost controls take effect. Even before your house is designed, you should have an idea whether your dreams will match your budget.

One of the reasons the 1997 Life Dream House seems so spacious is that the living and dining areas flow together. The kitchen and front entry, although screened from view, are open above to the same high ceiling as the living area. This makes a combined space of over 900 square feet. This is far more spacious than many homes that are twice as large and much more expensive.

Very little space is taken up by corridors and halls. We have asked all sorts of people who have toured the house to estimate its size. Invariably they think it is much larger than 2,100 square feet. Some have said it must be over 3,000 sq. ft. The recommended minimum lot size is 100 feet wide by 120 feet deep.

Here is the program that I developed for this house.

The 1997 Life Dream House

Notes of the requirements of the family.

- Family of four, parents and two children.
- Like to live informally most of the time.
- Living room to have a fireplace and high ceiling. Entertainment center.
- Dining table for four to expand to seat twelve on special occasions
- A covered porch at the rear that can be used for barbecue and outdoor dining.
- Kitchen to have cooktop and grille, convection oven, microwave oven, refrigerator, freezer, double sink, garbage disposal, trash compactor.
- Counter in kitchen for breakfast and snacks.
- Master suite, king-size bed and walk-in closet. French doors that open onto a private porch. Bathroom to have two lavatories, whirlpool tub, separate shower.
- A study/home office with desk, computer space, file cabinets, bookshelves.
- Two children's rooms, each with study desk, bookshelves, and window seat large enough to accommodate a sleepover friend.
- Children's bathroom to have tub/shower and two lavatories.
- Wall space to display art.
- Lots of storage space.
- Powder room.
- Laundry room.
- Two-car garage with workbench and storage space.
- Double-glazed windows.
- Wood floors, carpet in bedrooms, tile in kitchen and bathrooms.
- Family has two dogs.

Function Area *(Square Feet)*

The areas denote enclosed, heated (air-conditioned) space, measured from the inside face of exterior walls.

Entry	100
Living	500
Dining	170
Study/Guest/Nursery	110
Kitchen	196
Laundry/Mudroom	40
Powder Room	40
Master Bedroom	236
Master Bath/Dressing	130
Bedroom No. 2	200
Bedroom No. 3	200
Bath	64
Circulation	70
Mechanical	<u>40</u>
Total	2,100 sq. ft.

Spaces Not Heated or Cooled

Garage/Storage	580	2 cars, three bicycles
Outdoor Covered Porch	240	Space for outdoor dining for up to 16

As you proceed to prepare your own building program, list the various activities and opposite each write comments on how you will use the space and any of your special needs and conditions. Remember the proverb, *"Non multa sed mutum"* — not quantity but quality.

MAKING A BUBBLE DIAGRAM

After you have established this list, there is another step I suggest you should take before you start laying out the floor plan. Draw a simple bubble diagram (see illustration). This is not a complicated step and it will help you and your architect identify the various activities or functions of your home. By laying out a diagram of the flow of space you will be able to determine whether the various activities need to be connected or separated. Obviously, to get from the living area to the dining table you don't want to walk through a sleeping area. You need to have the kitchen accessible to deliveries and trash removal. You will want to consider the relationship of children's rooms to the master suite, and so forth.

Making a diagram of the functions of your home is the best way to plan it so that it serves you effectively.

Bubble diagram used to define the flow and functions of the House for Life.

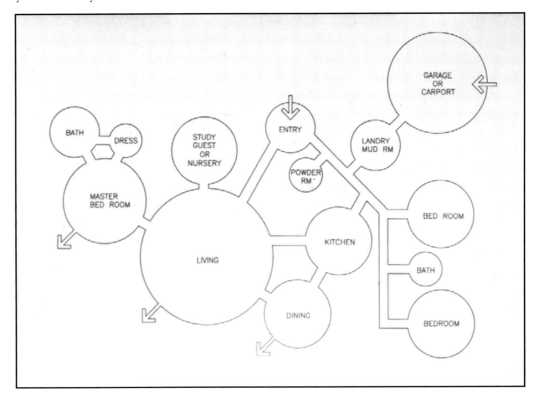

FITTING YOUR HOME TO ITS SITE

Get a map of your property. Standing on your site, approximately in the center of where the house will be, identify the view angles — ones you like and ones you consider undesirable. Draw some arrows on the map to show these.

There is other information, which your architect can help you to collect:

- If your site slopes, you will need a topographic map. This will be provided by a local civil engineer and your architect will specify the scale and contour intervals. The map should show the property lines and adjacent streets. If there are natural features such as trees, shrubs, rocks or drainage areas, they should be indicated. Check to be sure that you are not in the path of a future highway or utility corridor, or in a seismic zone or a fire hazard area. Check on noise from highways and airplane flight paths.

- Identify the solar angles — the summer sunrise and sunset, and winter sunrise and sunset. If the area is subject to winds or driving rain, note their direction and intensity. Investigate whether any privacy problems exist or are a potential for the future as the neighborhood develops.

A map that shows both the natural elements and man-made conditions of your property will have a major impact on the way your house is designed and oriented.

Today's dream is tomorrow's reality.

—William Shakespeare

Top: *Serenity means harmony with Nature.*

Above left: *Working with builders Russ and Brad Riggs.*

Above right: *Teamwork — client, architect, builder, apprentice.*

PLANNING
YOUR HOME

Skate to where the puck is going to be, not where it has been.

— Wayne Gretzky

Homo sapiens is the only species that makes plans to have, or not have, children, and then maintains a relationship, often close, between the members of its family. The connections may continue for much or most of their existence on earth. Our family is apt to be the primary motive for our actions in life. And although family usually denotes relatives through blood or marriage, it can also include an extended family of friends, colleagues or persons of similar interests.

Creating a beautiful and functional home is one of the most important and consequential acts you can do on behalf of your family. The quality of your home is constantly influencing the quality of your lives. Your family house should be both cozy and spacious. It should be warm and inviting, easy to maintain. It should be versatile enough to evolve as the family grows. Its design should be timeless. With the increased frenzy and fast pace of life, your family home should be the stable element that nurtures, unites and continues to inspire the members of your family.

Your home should be your sanctuary, the place where you and your family are safe from harm and stress.

What have we learned about how the beauty of a home can enhance our life and bring constant joy to our family? After a lifetime at Taliesin and discussions with families who live in a home designed according to organic principles, I know there is a profound quality to good architecture that does exactly that.

As all who have raised a family know, the first child to arrive creates a major shift in our

Opposite: *A seamless connection between indoors and outdoors.*

lives. It is an event for which we think we are quite prepared, only to discover that there is much to learn. The old scenario, with father away all day earning a living and mother at home cooking, cleaning and raising the children, is largely a thing of the past. Today, both parents may be wage earners. Since many businesses can be run from the house, you may both be home all day.

The arrival of a baby has a significant impact on life within our house. Playpens, clothes and toys are everywhere. Furniture is threatened, and itself becomes a threat to children, as they crash into a glass-topped coffee table, or find a drawer full of kitchen knives. There is a big increase in cleaning and maintenance, as the dangers of fire, electricity and hazardous chemicals take on a new light. Stairs become major hazards.

As we grow into adulthood, we forget what the world looks like to children. We want easy-to-clean surfaces, yet softer rather than harder. Almost nothing in a house is in scale with children. New parents should spend some time crawling around on the floor to see it from their child's point of view.

A home with two master suites honors your guests.

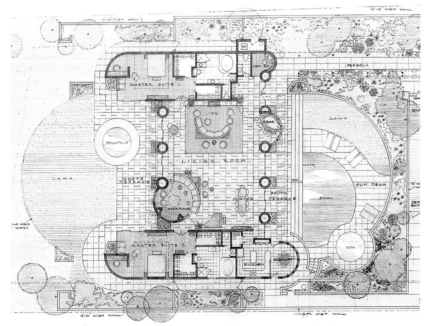

A child's room should be designed to a smaller scale. It should also be flexible enough to adjust for growth. A thoughtful house plan will consider the possibility of adding bedrooms for future children. If a young family of moderate means intends to have children, a good way to plan a home may be to add bedrooms later as the family expands. This possibility needs to be incorporated in the design, and your architect should help you plan ahead for maximum flexibility.

Eventually the time will come when your children grow up and leave home. Will you keep their room ready for their return? Will it accommodate two people when they get married? Planning the house for your family requires some

thought for the future. Is your family multi-generational? The time might also come when you invite your own parents to live with you. What happens if one of you becomes incapacitated? No plan will cover every eventuality, but the more thought you put into these matters and the more flexibility you incorporate, the more effective your house will become.

A home needs to serve individuals and it also needs to be communal — serving your family and your guests. Since the concept of family is so basic to the purpose of life, it would follow that the home should be thoughtfully designed to support and enhance the various family activities. You might ask yourself these questions:

- Is my house designed to specifically serve my family's needs?
- Does it inspire us daily with its beauty?
- Does it nurture each member of my family?
- Is it in human scale, so that its proportions relate to the members of my family, including our children?
- Is my front door scaled to the size of a human being or is it scaled to size of the developer or real estate agent's ego?
- Do I need to accommodate a Greyhound bus outside my front door?

Space that is intimate yet spacious for entertaining.

55

Architecture should grace the landscape.

If you have a large, tall entry hall, ask yourself if it was designed to serve the needs of your family, who use it the most, or your guests, who use it less frequently. Or was it perhaps designed so that the real estate agent who showed you through could exclaim about the drama of the entry experience. If your house is in the moderate-cost range, are you sacrificing living space for an extravagant entry?

How much of your house is really designed to help this agent clinch the sale? How much is your house designed to impress the neighbors rather than to support your family? For a family with a moderate income to spend its hard-earned money to show off to the neighborhood seems less important than creating an environment that raises the level of quality of life for those who live within.

The house grows out of its site.

To properly serve you, your house should be designed to fit your own specific needs, to support your family's particular and unique lifestyle. Have you ever sat down together and made a list of what is most important to each one of you and arrived at a consensus? What are your priorities? Have you thought about what your ideal home, your dream house, would be like? These are the sort of questions that an architect needs to ask you, and that people designing houses on "spec" (speculatively — not to order) should be asking themselves.

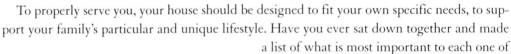
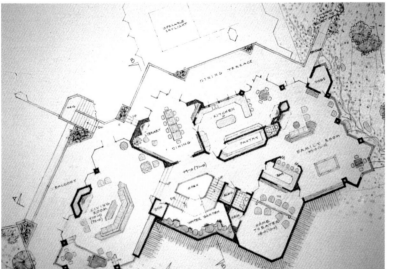

In the Victorian house, guests were entertained in the parlor. The parlor was gradually replaced by the living room, a space seldom used by the family except at Thanksgiving and other special occasions. The furniture was covered with doilies and antimacassars so it would not get soiled, and although it was called a living room, not much living was done there. How different are our lifestyles today. We are much more informal. Most young people in America have more spare time than their parents and grandparents did when they were growing up. We have learned to relax, to become less formal, more comfortable. In its role of nurturing the family, a house needs to accommodate the sort of things we do in our leisure time.

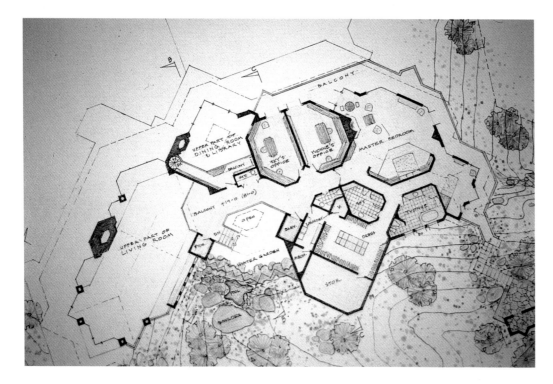

The plan is oriented to capture panoramic views.

We need appropriate space for entertaining our family, which usually includes television as well as space for entertaining friends and guests. Most of these occasions involve food, the most ancient way for humans to welcome guests. Social occasions can extend from a few people to an extensive gathering, a sit-down dinner or a backyard barbecue. Many houses today have both a living room and a family room. For a moderate-size house this means that the family spends its time in the family room and uses the living room to entertain guests. Budget limitations will limit the size of these rooms.

The trend today is towards building bigger and bigger houses. Fifty years ago, the average size of a house in Phoenix was 1,100 square feet for a family of five. Today the average size is 2,200 sq. ft. for a family of three, and twenty percent of the houses being built are over 3,000 sq. ft.

Rather than thinking, "How big?" we should be thinking, "How spacious?" When people walk through a well-designed house they remark on how spacious it seems. When they are informed of the actual square footage, they are incredulous. The house may be only half the size of the one in which they live, yet it seems much larger.

The reason is almost no wasted "space." No oversized entry hall, no long corridors, efficient kitchen and bathrooms, and reach-in rather than walk-in closets. Dining and living spaces are not separate rooms but spaces that flow together. An open plan with free flowing space makes your home seem much bigger. Building a house with a lot of wasted or ineffective space is a good way to throw away your money. If you built smaller, but with more sense

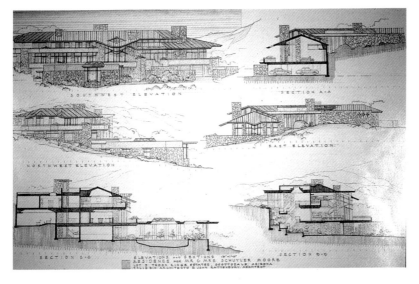

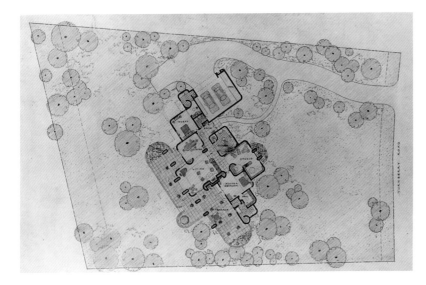

Top: *In tune with its desert environment.*

Above: *A two-bedroom home for an artist.*

of space, you can afford a higher level of quality.

We make "waste" space a part of the house; make it so beautiful it is not wasted. It is something like the little boy eating an apple, and another little boy ranges up alongside and wants to know if he can have the core, but the apple-eater says, "Sorry, there ain't gonna be no core."

In the moderate-cost house, rather than providing three separate rooms for living, dining and family, it makes more sense to provide one generous space. A single space instead of three separate rooms means less cleaning, less furniture, less maintenance and lower energy costs.

For larger homes, there are special spaces, such as a home theater. An ultimate luxury, it has large-screen video projection, surround sound, luxurious seating and a bar/kitchenette. In the moderate-size home, the living area can be furnished to serve nicely as your home theater.

Another possibility for children is a playroom, a place where they can play games and hold parties. A small stage for live performances is a nice feature. There are two aspects to consider. The space should be located so that guests can come and go without interrupting adults, and noise should be contained. In the moderate-size home, the covered porch serves as a play area in good weather, and children's bedrooms are large enough for play and study as well as sleeping.

Life expectancy has increased significantly in the past hundred years, partly due to improved health care. As we become more health conscious and appreciate the benefits of staying physically fit, many people participate in fitness programs, both physical and spiritual. Many homes today include an exercise or meditation room. Homes in the sunshine states usually have swimming pools, even an indoor pool. A space saver is the short pool with a moving current of water that can be adjusted to the speed of the swimmer. A more affordable solution for children is an inflatable plastic pool.

Larger homes may have tennis courts. We have designed houses with indoor squash courts and gymnasiums. In the moderate-size home, recreation may be limited to an exercise bicycle, walking/running treadmill or other types of workout machines that take up little space. Placing the machine in front of a window with a view out and the possibility of fresh air will make the circumstance much more pleasant. Computer golf can take place in a small room. Balls are hit into a net, and a computer analyzes the strength, spin and direction of the ball (even though it only travels a few feet) and calculates where it would have gone on a golf course.

For some, there are lots of other ways to get exercise around the house. Gardening is a good way to get exercise, fresh air and create beauty. A do-it-yourselfer can get exercise by maintaining and improving the home. Many people have hobbies, and want space for their activity. We should remember that the word "recreation" means to re-create oneself. A beautiful home is going to do a lot in this regard.

And if we are to have a healthy life we need a healthy house. For example, nothing has yet replaced the window that opens to admit fresh air. Many of the building products on the market today are made with noxious chemicals. The only way to avoid constantly inhaling their fumes is to provide cross ventilation and introduce fresh air from outdoors (assuming that the air quality in your neighborhood is still good).

Great minds discuss ideas, average minds discuss events, small minds discuss people.
—Alicia Bristow

Plasticity of form responds to the human shape.

FAMILY ACTIVITIES

Whenever possible, keep it simple. Simplicity is the ultimate sophistication.

—Leonardo da Vinci

Here are some thoughts on the various activities and spaces you may want in your home. They were all fundamental to my thinking when I designed the Dream House for *Life* magazine in 1997. I distilled all my experience designing homes into a simple plan based on common sense.

Opposite: *Sidelights bring in natural daylight.*

As I worked on the idea, I felt some concern over calling it a Dream House, since I wanted it to be more than a dream. When a timely opportunity arose to build the house before it was published, I began to refer to it as "A House for Life."

The goal was to create a moderate-cost home that responds to the needs of the average American family. This is a challenge in itself, if you believe, as I do, that no person really wants to be regarded as either average or ordinary. In addition to *Life* magazine's requirements, I wanted the plan flexible so it could be built with two, three or four bedrooms. Most of the rooms are capable of expansion.

The design has some guiding principles:

- Humanize the house — keep it in human scale, use natural materials, warm colors.
- Nurture the family — with beauty, comfort and excitement.
- Give the house a spiritual quality — this is what we find in Nature.
- Create a timeless design — don't follow a "style" that will soon be out of style.
- Make it flexible — spaces may need to be expanded, contracted or used differently.

Because families are spending less time together, what with work, school, sports and other activities that take them away from home, a house should be designed to help unite and nurture them during the times they are together.

The plan of the House for Life is adaptable to all types of families — unmarried, married with children, married without children, mixed generations and retired. It is designed to meet the ever-changing needs of your family. It can start out as a two-bedroom house, with more bedrooms being added when needed and as funds permit. The plan is adaptable, and of the hundreds of houses around the country that have been built using this design, some are on sloping sites and some are on suburban lots. While some sites have views, others have none, just neighbors on all sides.

The side-opening garage is much preferred over the front-opening type. However, if your lot is narrow, the plan will allow the garage door to face the street.

Five different roof forms are available to suit individual tastes and fit different climates and neighborhoods — in any part of North America. For narrow lots, there is a two-story model. The parents' room is separated from the children's, and there is a multi-purpose room that can serve as a nursery, a home office or a spare bedroom.

Understand that my goal is not to change the way you live, but to improve the home in which you live.

THE TYPES OF ACTIVITIES AND SPACES IN YOUR HOME

Entry Space

Most builder houses have the front door right in the middle and intentionally impressive. I recommend that, instead of trying to dazzle the neighbors with your entrance, you spend your hard-earned income on the inside. This is where your family lives. My favorite Spanish philosopher, Baltazaar Gracian, said, "Some houses have the portico of a palace leading to the rooms of a cottage."

The arrival experience should start out with a sense of human scale, then gradually increase in drama. You can do something special with the design of your front door but don't make it too big. Three feet wide by seven feet high is large enough. Double entrance doors are a waste of space and money in a modest-size home. Remember that the first part of your home that anyone actually touches is the doorknob. A hardwood knob is friendlier than a metal one.

Keep the entry, or reception area, modest in size. You

spend a lot more time in the other rooms of your house. Give first priority to your family. Screen the living area so that your guests won't walk right in on you. Plan the entrance experience so that it builds up to a crescendo rather than starts with one. A little mystery adds charm to your home. Bring daylight into this area (with sidelights or a skylight) and be sure there is a roof over the guests who are standing at your door waiting to come in. A full-length mirror in the entry area gives you (and your guests) a way to check your appearance as you enter or leave. It also helps make the small space seem larger.

The front door to the House for Life opens into a reception area that leads to either the living area or the kitchen. The members of your family will usually enter through the garage. After passing through the laundry/mudroom, you come into the reception area.

Door knocker — every detail is considered.

Garage or Carport

The garage in the House for Life accommodates two vehicles (a car and an SUV, pickup, or minivan). It has space for a workbench and storage. A separate door allows you to come and go without using the overhead door. The garage is designed as a wing of the house. This allows it to be built as a three- or four-car garage (or be enlarged in the future). The garage floor is sloped to drain out under the overhead door. It steps up at the point where the front wheels should stop, so as to prevent you from running into the back wall at two o'clock in the morning.

A fireplace is a good focal point for the living room.

Bottom: *Spaciousness is more important than size.*

Living, Family and Entertaining Space

This is the space where you will live as a family and entertain your friends and guests. If your income is moderate, you should spend it judiciously. In terms of spaciousness, this area should be generous in size. Instead of providing both a family room and a living room, consider just one large space that will serve adequately for both family use and entertaining guests.

The living area should be the most significant space in your home, designed to be informal and inviting. In the House for Life, it has long diagonal dimensions, space that flows around corners, and glass doors that open onto the covered porch. Because it is spatially linked to the dining area and the kitchen it is spacious and appears to be much larger than it really is.

Your living room should be proportioned to be comfortable for just a few people, but should also work for those occasions when many of your family and friends are gathered together. When the first model of the House for Life was completed at Gold Mountain, we hosted a welcome party for everybody who helped build it. There were seventy people in the house and on the covered porch but we didn't feel crowded.

The focal point of the home is a generous masonry fireplace. Next to this is a comfortable seating space for as many as ten people. The arrangement is designed to be cozy and friendly, facilitating the art of conversation. The ceiling is high in this area, and clerestory windows (a band of windows located near the ceiling, usually above a lower roof and below a higher roof) on either side provide an even balance of natural daylight. At night, light coves provide soft, indirect lighting. On one side of the fireplace, hidden behind cabinet doors, is the entertainment center with video and audio equipment. A family can enjoy the comforts of a home theater right in their living space.

The living area opens onto a multi-purpose area, a study or home office

The living room ceiling is highest at the fireplace.

that can also serve as a library, guest bedroom or a nursery. French doors open onto a generous covered porch and provide natural cross ventilation.

A living room should be as comfortable for two as it is for ten.

Dining Space

Mealtimes provide a variety of ways for a family to get together. In the House for Life, the dining area is a separate space but not a separate room. It is an alcove adjacent to the living area and open to the kitchen. It has a semi-circular bay window with a view of the garden. The dining table is round so everybody can easily see each other and converse. The table normally seats

six but can be expanded to seat twelve for special occasions. Because the area is informal it can more readily be used between meals. The table is useful for other purposes.

For snacks, there is an eighteen-inch-wide ledge that is set lower than the counter. The dining chairs work here as well as for the dining table.

There are other places where the family can eat — in the

Warm colors and natural materials help make a house a home.

A boat-shaped table makes conversation easier.

65

A change in level (up or down) gives a dining space its own individuality.

The space is in scale when people are seated.

living area (if they want to watch TV) or on the outdoor covered porch and barbecue area. Dining out has less appeal with more options at home.

Cooking Space

The kitchen is the heart of the home and should be configured for maximum efficiency, with everything within easy reach. In the House for Life, an island table gives the cook's helpers a place to work (the space above it is an ideal location for a pot rack). There are lots of built-in cabinets and one entire wall is devoted to a reach-in pantry and storage cabinets.

The countertops and backsplashes are Corian and the nosing is the same material with a wood inlay. The narrow shelf at the top of the backsplash is for spices. A sit-down counter allows for informal meals. The kitchen can be opened to the living space or closed off with a simple wood shutter. This allows the cook to converse with people in the living area or watch the same TV.

Remember that the kitchen, with its appliances, plumbing fixtures and cabinets, is the most expensive space to build. It is also a high-maintenance area that calls for daily cleaning. All more reasons to keep it small and efficient.

The kitchen in the House for Life has a view of the backyard, where the children play. The floor plan is designed so that the kitchen and dining areas can be switched.

A circular kitchen designed to make cooking easier.

Note that the cabinets are quite simple. The doors and drawers are "flush front" rather than panelized, and the hardware is also very simple. In the corner cabinets a lazy-susan turntable can be installed to save space and make things accessible.

Right: The kitchen hood is an integral part of the design.

All appliances eventually wear out. Since new and presumably better models are constantly appearing on the market, kitchens should be designed so that appliances are easy to remove and replace. We should be able to unplug and replace an oven or a cooktop. In the future we should be able to "unplug" an entire kitchen or bathroom and plug in a new one. The old one will go to a recycling factory.

Every year, the major manufacturers of

kitchen and laundry appliances come out with new models. Part of the fun of building a new house is going to the showrooms and seeing the latest products. By the time you start to do this you should have decided whether you want to use gas or electricity as a fuel, or perhaps both.

I think appliance showrooms should set up a model kitchen and allow you to actually cook or wash something. You should be allowed to "test drive" a product before you decide. Failing this, go see the model homes in a new development in your area, or find a friend who has just put in a new kitchen.

To store your minor appliances — mixers, blenders, toasters and so forth — consider the possibility of an appliance garage, a storage cabinet at counter height with a roll-down door.

Most appliances come in a choice of colors. White is traditional but I suggest you consider another color. Stainless steel or brushed chrome will not clash. Some brands of refrigerators and freezers can have wood panels inserted in the doors. If your kitchen is open to your dining area or family room, this is a good way to harmonize the spaces.

A kitchen that takes advantage of panoramic views.

A window seat or bed for sleepover guests converts to a desktop.

Above right: Your choice: study, home office, nursery, hobby room or guest bedroom.

Pullout plastic bins will provide for trash and recycling, and you should have separate containers for metal, glass and paper.

I suggest you include a small desk and space for storing cookbooks. The desk should be large enough to accommodate a telephone, directories and a laptop computer, with a shelf below for a printer. If you don't have a home office, this could be the place you sort mail, pay bills and keep your calendar. It is a good place for family communications and might include a mail center, with cubbyholes for each member of the family (a better solution than hanging messages on the refrigerator with magnets). You will not regret providing adequate storage space in this area.

Multi-Purpose Space

A key to the success of a moderate-size house is providing an area that can be used for more than one purpose. On the side of the living area in the House for Life is a space that can be used for a variety of activities. It is normally open to the living area but can be closed off with a pocket or folding door. This space can serve as a home office. It can be a library/study. It might be a sewing or hobby room. It can serve as a spare bedroom. It can also be used as a nursery when the children are very young (it is located next to the master bedroom). When it is used as an office, the round shape allows for a wrap-around desk.

Recreational Space

If your budget allows, you may want to include a space for indoor recreational activities, such as table tennis, pool or billiards, cards, electronic games and so forth. Some families have special needs, such as a "stage" for children to present a play or a musical performance. The floor might be used for dancing, so wood is a good choice. Think what you might use this space for after the children have grown up.

Sleeping Spaces

This bedroom includes an alcove and doors that open onto a terrace.

Parents usually want to be near their children while they are babies, and the nursery allows for this. But the time quickly comes when both parents and children want some degree of separation. The plan for the House for Life includes layouts for two, three or four bedrooms. It is arranged so that parents are on one side of the home and children are on the other.

The master suite has a bay window with built-in seat large enough to sleep on, a bathroom with double sinks, tub and separate shower, and a walk-in closet. It has its own private, covered porch (large enough for outdoor sleeping).

The basic model has two children's bedrooms, each with a bay window with a seat large enough to accommodate a sleepover guest. A built-in desk provides a place for them to do homework. Wardrobe closets are located so as to act as a sound block between the two rooms.

Some couples, as they grow older, may want separate bedrooms. After the children have grown up and left, their rooms can be converted into a second master suite.

Bathrooms

Today's trend is to build enormous, luxurious bathrooms. Even people with a modest budget are lured into splurging on costly plumbing fixtures and extravagant accessories. Frank Lloyd Wright's attitude, no doubt influenced by the decline and fall of the Roman Empire, was that bathroom functions should be done quickly and efficiently. Better to spend your time and money in and on the rest of your home. Avoid the gold-plated accessories and semi-precious stone insets. Next to the kitchen, this is the second most expensive space to build, even without such extravagances. Since it is also a high-maintenance area, in a moderate-cost home it should be small and efficient.

Opposite left: Tables for cards and pool, electronic games.

Opposite center: Pool table has custom light fixtures.

Opposite right: Children's game room with dance floor.

Below left: Children's snack bar.

Below center: Tree house for children (and adults).

Below right: The fence that encloses the swimming pool echoes the design theme.

Lower platform beds are generally more comfortable than higher box spring beds.

Above right: A drawer below the bed provides useful storage.

In the House for Life plan, the master bath has both a walk-in shower and a tub. The children have a tub/shower combination. The separate shower is highly recommended, and can be a premanufactured unit or custom-built. The snail shower is a good solution since its spiral configuration eliminates the need for a shower door or curtain.

Be sure to have a thermostatically controlled shower valve. Most people today take a shower to get clean and use a tub for soaking and relaxing. A Jacuzzi tub may be a worthwhile luxury. Remember to provide a grab bar you can hold onto while getting out of the tub. A seat that folds down from the wall is useful.

The master bath has twin lavatories mounted in a countertop. The countertop is set thirty-three inches high, which is higher than the standard thirty-one inches and more comfortable for most adults to use. The cabinet below provides for storage, as does the cabinet on the wall behind the water closet. A simple and effective medicine cabinet is one that mounts over the

A tub with a view of an enclosed garden.

sink and has three mirrors. The ones on the side swing to create a three-way mirror. Mirrors are an effective way to make a space appear larger.

In colder climates you might consider electric radiant heating in the floor.

Laundry

The best place for the laundry is not too far from the bedrooms or kitchen, so in the House for Life it is combined with the mudroom. Washer and dryer are next to each other, but a stacked unit would save on space. A retractable clothesline accommodates drip/dry clothes (the room has a floor drain). A sorting and folding table is provided, with storage underneath for detergents, dirty clothes and linen. An ironing board folds into the wall. Many people will prefer to do their ironing and sewing in the living/family room or on the porch.

Home Office

Many people now work full- or part-time at home. They enjoy the quiet atmosphere, the ability to be near their family, flexible work hours and no office rent, as well as the time saved by not commuting. On the other hand, the home-worker may be more easily distracted. There are both advantages and disadvantages to consider.

If you want to include a home office there are many possibilities. You can use the study/guest nursery or one of the bedrooms, if you have a spare; or you can add another room, possibly a detached structure. You will need space for a desk, computer, filing cabinets and shelves. Some families want home-office space for both parents.

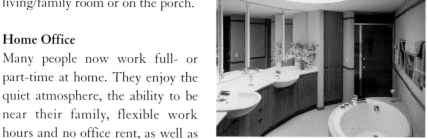

Home School

There is a growing trend towards home schooling. It is estimated that some two million families in the U.S. are teaching their children at home. The prime reason is a conviction that they can provide a better education than the schools are doing. The idea is endorsed by William Bennett, the former U.S. Secretary of Education. It has produced some brilliant and successful people. Thomas Edison, William Blake, Jean-Jacques Rousseau and Frank Lloyd Wright were all home-schooled.

Ideally you would have a space at home that is dedicated to this educational use. You will need space for desks, shelves, wall surfaces and good lighting.

It is better to know some of the questions than all of the answers.

–James Thurber

THE BUDGET

Why waste good livable space with an attic or basement? Never plan waste space with the idea of eventually converting it into rooms. A house that is planned with a lot of space to be used some other day is not likely to be a well-planned house.

— FLLW

It is a fact that almost everybody who builds a house, especially for the first time, will end up spending more than they had originally anticipated. There are several reasons for this. The first is not taking into consideration all of the items involved. In addition to the "hard" costs, such as land, utilities, construction, landscaping, and furnishings, there are "soft" costs.

Soft costs include the cost of financing your home. There will be fees for attorneys, real estate agents, the title company, a soil analysis, and surveying. There will be fees for the architect, landscape architect, interior designer, engineers (civil, mechanical, electrical) and perhaps special consultants such as lighting or kitchen designers. There will be costs to purchase and comply with regulations, filing fees, a building permit, and course-of-construction insurance.

When you have considered each and every cost, you have created a Project Budget, which is more comprehensive than a Construction Budget. Comprehensive cost controls should be in place from start to finish and should be a prime concern of your architect and builder.

When a family starts to put aside money to build their house, one of the first things to come up is the question of costs. If you ask an architect, builder or real estate agent, you should be able to depend on their figures — these people are in the business. But they have a tendency to suggest construction costs that are, at the best, optimistically low. Remember that they are looking for business and they know that their competitors will probably quote on the low side.

To compound the problem, the construction industry doesn't make it clear how a cost estimate is defined. If you hear a figure of $150 per square foot, for example, you have to identify whether this applies to "livable area" (measured from the inside face of the exterior walls), or whether it is "gross area," measured to the outside face of the exterior walls. Builders and realtors always measure gross area.

As a homeowner, you think of livable area as the floor space that you can utilize. However, you are still going to have to pay for the area occupied by interior and exterior walls. The livable area may be ten to twenty percent smaller than the gross area.

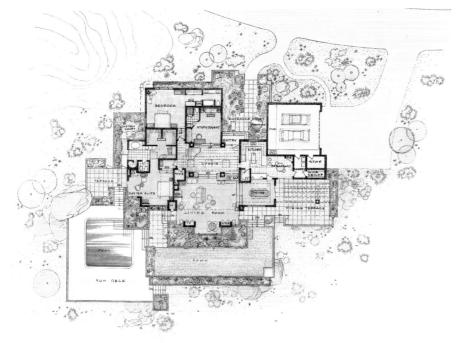

The guest room/study has a folding wall which can normally be left open.

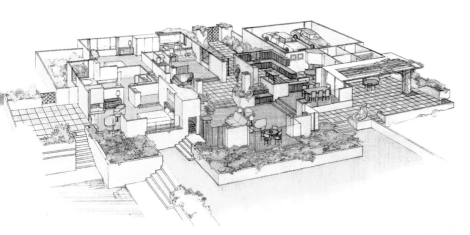

The 3D view of the interior is easier for most people to comprehend.

Be sure that you are clear regarding the budget for the garage or carport. Not all builders use the same rules regarding this space. You will probably have other features — walks, steps, terraces, gardens, walls or fences, perhaps a pool. Be sure these items are accounted for in the budget.

Construction costs vary significantly from city to city, county to county and state to state. There will be cost differences between an urban area, the suburbs and the countryside. Costs also constantly fluctuate with the economy and the availability of materials and labor. From the time when you first to start to plan your home to the time when you receive firm bids, there may be an increase in the cost of labor and materials.

A surprise often comes when a builder starts to charge you an "extra cost" for items that were not included in the contract. An example would be if you wanted to make a room larger, change a door or upgrade the quality of your roof after construction commenced. In this highly competitive industry, some builders rely heavily on profits made by charging for "extras." When you sign a contract, you should have your attorney review it, and you should pay close attention to how much markup will be charged for "extras."

When you are budgeting for your new house, be sure to include insurance premiums during construction. If your house burns down before you move in, are you covered? What happens if your builder goes broke before he finishes the job? What happens if one of the subcontractors defaults? What does your contract say about the consequences of your builder not finishing within the agreed-upon time period?

You should also be careful that your contract with the builder spells out how much he is going to charge for overhead and profit for any changes you want to make after construction has started. These figures are almost sure to be higher than what was charged for the original contract.

Sometimes things get omitted from budgets, such as the cost of plan copies, building permits, built-in cabinets and security systems. It is the responsibility of an architect to protect

you from these problems. To a large extent it comes down to a matter of trust, which means that you should select both your architect and builder with the greatest of care. Get the names of their other clients and call them up, visit their homes. Reputable architects or builders should furnish you with the names of *all* their clients, not just a careful selection of names of those whom they are confident will have favorable things to say.

Your budget should include some contingency funds. This is to cover unforeseen events, labor strikes, weather problems and other circumstances you cannot control.

Many people are concerned about the resale value of their house. Consequently, in the process of designing a new home, they may want to give some thought to rooms or features that they don't need but which they believe will be attractive to a future buyer. But this should not lead to building a house that has been designed for somebody else rather than for one's own family.

The street side is quiet and unpretentious.

Living, dining, kitchen and master bedroom are open to the view side.

The covered porch extends the living space and allows for outdoor dining.

Variations of the 1997 Life Dream House at Gold Mountain have been built all over the U.S.

There are many poor ways to save money in the construction of your home, especially

• stinting on the footings and foundations;
• not insulating properly;
• not investing in a good roofing system.

All the things in your house and the house itself are at risk from water damage. Being thrifty by using cheaper roofing or waterproofing systems is surely shortsighted. The initial cost of a quality roof is likely to be a fraction of the cost of repairs to water-damaged interiors and personal possessions. Areas that need special attention are where chimneys or walls project above roofs, and at valleys where roof slopes intersect. These areas should be flashed, and this is not a place to use cheap materials. Engaging an independent roofing consultant is a wise investment. If you can't find one, a good independent construction consultant is your next choice.

Many people think that one of the easiest ways to save money is to bypass the architect and use a standard builder plan, or perhaps a modification of a builder plan. The responsibility of a good architect is to produce a design that meets and exceeds the expectations of the client, and to provide a professional service that guards against costly problems during construction.

When you start to establish your project budget, I suggest that you make a checklist of all the items that will be involved. It is better to know the full cost up front rather than after the fact. A good architect and a good builder will not mind spending time on a careful explanation of costs, and will help you with cost controls. After all, their reputation is on the line.

The main questions that arise when one considers what to build have to do with quantity, quality and cost. It is the role of the architect, working with the builder, to carefully guide the

Nurture the family, help make them want to spend more time together.

Gable roofs are less expensive than hip roofs.

design and construction process so that the client gets as much quantity and quality as possible for the budget. Building a home is probably the single biggest monetary investment that a family makes. From the start of this adventure, it is wise to remember a simple equation that involves three factors:

$$Quantity \times Quality = Cost$$

In other words, the cost of construction is a result of the size of a house (the quantity) multiplied by the quality of its materials and workmanship.

Any two factors of this equation, when multiplied together, will result in the third factor. This means that Quantity × Cost = Quality, or Quality × Cost = Quantity.

If you have a fixed budget, as most people do, and feel that you must have a house of a certain size, then that will determine the level of quality that you can afford. If you want a higher level of quality, you are going to have to either reduce the size of the house or increase your budget.

But if you decide that your house must be larger, you may have to accept a lower standard of quality. This might mean, for instance, using stucco instead of stone, or less expensive kitchen appliances. If stone or higher-grade appliances are more important to you, you will have to find a way to make the house smaller.

If you increase either quantity or quality, you will increase cost. This is why it is essential to define your priorities.

One of the best ways to keep the size of a house under control is to design it so as to minimize corridors. Another is to let one space flow into another space.

The traditional method of constructing a new home is to have an architect prepare a design and then get several builders to quote competitive prices. Usually the lowest bidder is selected. However, this process has a serious flaw: *the lowest cost may not be your best bet.* Unless owner, architect and builder are all working in harmony, the results may be in question. A good way to solve the problem of staying within your budget and schedule is to have your architect and builder working together from the start. This is the premise of the design/build program, which provides a single source of responsibility for the design and construction of your home. The design/build team guides the homeowner through the wide variety of tasks that are involved from the time you decide to build up until the time you move in.

The team can assist you to select and acquire a site and recommend ways to obtain financing. Services include the custom design, construction, landscaping and furnishings of your home. Cost controls are exercised from start to finish. It is the most intelligent way to realize your dream of a new home with a minimum of problems, and to ensure that you receive the quality you are paying for (while relieving you of responsibilities you don't need).

Beauty rests on necessities. The line of beauty is the result of perfect economy. The cell of the bee is built at that angle which gives it the most strength with the least wax; the bone or quill of the bird give the most alar strength with the least weight. There is not a particle to spare in natural structure.

—Ralph Waldo Emerson

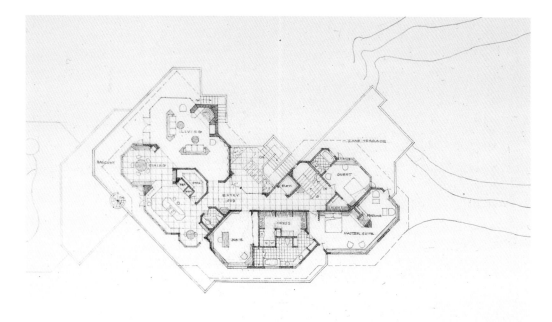

Floor plan of the Myers House.

*The challenge is to design a home for
a family with a modest income.*

THE MODERATE-COST HOUSE

The house of moderate cost is not only America's major architectural problem but the problem most difficult for her major architects. As for me, I would rather solve it with satisfaction than build anything I can think of.

— FLLW

In my career I have designed many homes for affluent people. In some cases the budget was a secondary consideration — it was more important to create a design that not only met their requirements but inspired their imagination. A different sort of challenge comes with the prospect of designing a home for a family of more modest means.

We have long known how to plan homes that are sensible, efficient, spacious, flexible and perfectly suited to their site and the needs of the owner, houses with free, open space, rather than the confinement of a box. A house can have all these qualities and still be built at a moderate cost.

Then why is it that so many of the houses being built in America today completely lack these attributes? Why does our home, the personal environment in which we live and raise our family, seem to have so little individuality or integrity? Why does it cost so much and waste so much space? Why does our house look like so many other people's houses?

The problem starts with education. Architecture is a subject that is omitted from most people's education. It is our blind spot. We learn little about architecture from our parents or in school. We learn about mathematics and science, art and the humanities. We learn languages, psychology, and medicine, how to conduct business and how to make money. We learn about politics, sports and entertainment, about telephones, television, and computers.

But although we spend most of the waking and sleeping hours of our lives in and around architecture, although our man-made environment has an enormous influence on our health, happiness and our ability to work or relax more effectively, most of us know little about what

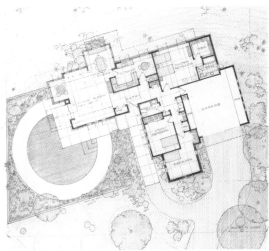

constitutes good architecture. If we did, we would not tolerate the unsightly buildings that surround us, ugliness that we continue to build every day. The only saving grace of many houses today are the trees, bushes and vines that are planted around them. Our houses are, for the most part, far behind the times.

The great majority of houses are not designed by architects. There are several reasons for this. The first problem lies with architects themselves. Many regard designing a residence as requiring a great deal of effort in relation to the compensation received. They can make more money, more easily, by designing commercial or institutional structures.

If relatively few architects design houses, then who does establish the pattern of residential design? Would you believe that the biggest influence on the design of houses are the people who sell real estate!

This moderate-cost home has a two-story living room.

How is this possible? Well, the majority of new homes are not custom designed for a particular client or for a specific site but are built on speculation by developers. A typical housing development will have a half dozen models from which a buyer may choose. These standard house plans are copied from another housing project, which in turn is a copy of a copy. The plans were probably drawn by a draftsperson who works for the developer.

Since the driving motive is to make as much money as possible, in the shortest time, with the lowest possible risk, there is little incentive for developers to rethink a house design or to build something better. The money-clock is running and it is always hungry. So "new" models will get fancy names, together with descriptions that make them sound like a mansion or a palace. These "new" models may feature some different ornamental decorations, and they will surely have the newest line of appliances, but the basic design will be a reiteration of what sold last year.

If you look at the average spec house (a house built "speculatively" rather than to order) of today and compare it to the spec house of your grandparents' time, you will see little evolution. Today's house may have the latest kitchen appliances, television and a super security sys-

If your lot is narrow, three stories may be needed.

Opposite: *Detaching the garage allows for an enclosed garden at the entry.*

tem; it may have a porte cochère (a covered entrance from the drive to the doorway) and a big garage. Otherwise it pretty much follows the patterns of the past. The design of houses doesn't change much around the country, even though the climate, terrain and vegetation may be vastly different. We see the same house designs on the coast of New England, in the forests of Montana and the deserts of Arizona.

When we buy a new car, we expect a more advanced model every year. And beyond the basic model we demand lots of options. We don't take this attitude with housing. A spec house may offer a few choices or additional features but this is the exception rather than the rule. Options are often limited to the type of kitchen appliances or the color of paint.

An overhead trellis adds charm and helps the scale.

Why do real estate agents have an enormous impact on house design? For those concerned with making money in selling residential real estate, the most important moment in the deal comes when the prospective buyer enters the house. Look at it from the sales point-of-view. Agents have to "sell" the features of this house to the prospective buyer. Knowing the importance of a first impression, they want something that will impress the buyer the moment they approach the house. So what could be more impressive that an enormous porte cochère. Never mind that most people will not drive through it (in many cases you cannot). It must be big, it must send out a message: "I am as important, as successful, as my neighbor."

Not so many years ago, American automobiles used to do this. They got bigger and bigger, had enormous tail fins, massive radiator grilles, and everything was outlined in chrome. Well, thanks to European and Japanese car manufacturers who designed smaller, more functional and more beautiful cars at competitive prices, Detroit finally had to change its ways. What we need in America is this sort of awakening regarding our houses.

In the past one hundred years we have seen some amazing changes. We have invented the radio, television, computers, and the Internet. We have explored outer space and put people on the moon. We have found cures for a host of diseases and extended our lifespan. We have split the atom. We have fought for freedom and encouraged democracy over much of the world.

What have we done for our homes? Most of us still live in the same sort of box as our grandparents lived in. Although there are some architects and builders who work diligently to create better houses, the public is largely unaware of their work.

When an automobile or an airplane manufacturer decides to put out a new model, they have a design department (backed up by a research and development department) that has a reasonable budget and time period to create a new model. The designers prepare many sketches and make models that are tested in wind tunnels and with sophisticated computer programs.

The housing industry, on the other hand, produces few new ideas or fresh designs. Why bother, when it can just take last year's

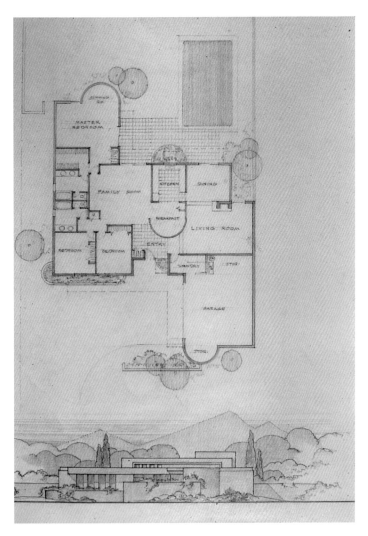

A three-bedroom house on a 65-foot-wide lot.

model, tweak the façade and give it a different name? Research and development is skipped over because there is no substantive and unified R & D department for housing. Why would we need it if the public seems perfectly content with what it has now?

It is about time that we woke up. As long as there is such a demand for housing that the industry can make money without improving anything, and as long as the public stays blind to the fact that we should demand something better, families will continue to be confined to living in unhealthy, unattractive boxes.

There is a better alternative. A moderate-cost house can be both functional and beautiful. An effective plan, although quite small in size, will have a sense of spaciousness. It is usually more comfortable than a large house. A smaller space results in lower construction costs, lower utility bills, fewer furnishings and less maintenance. A beautiful house will not only inspire the family who lives there but will appreciate in value beyond the norm. A beautiful house enhances the neighborhood.

Many years ago Frank Lloyd Wright asked, "What is the matter with the typical American house? Well, it lies about everything. It has no sense of unity at all nor any such sense of space as should belong to a free people. Stuck up in thoughtless fashion, the thing is more a hive than a home. It has no appropriate sense of proportion, it's a bedeviled box with a fussy lid."

We might well pose the same question today and arrive at a similar answer.

Wright was one of the few architects who not only designed sensible, moderate-cost houses but also devised new methods to construct them. Over a period of some fifty years, he pursued a variety of ideas for designing and building a home for a family with a modest income. Despite large commissions that came his way his interest in creating moderate-cost homes remained undiminished.

Continuing the effort to design a moderate-cost home, Taliesin Architects worked with the National Homes Corporation in 1971 to design a diverse line of manufactured houses, ranging from mobile and modular units to duplexes and ranch houses.

Some years later I created a line of mobile homes for the International Homes Corporation of Arizona. The plans featured angular ends with mitered windows. When two units were connected side by side they provided a generous interior space.

In 1980, I designed a production home for Ross Roll. He owned a company in Mesa that manufactured Perlite, a lightweight cellular insulating material that could be added to concrete to make it an "insulating concrete." The walls and roof of the house were all made of poured-in-place Perlite concrete. After the house was built, the metal forms could be reused.

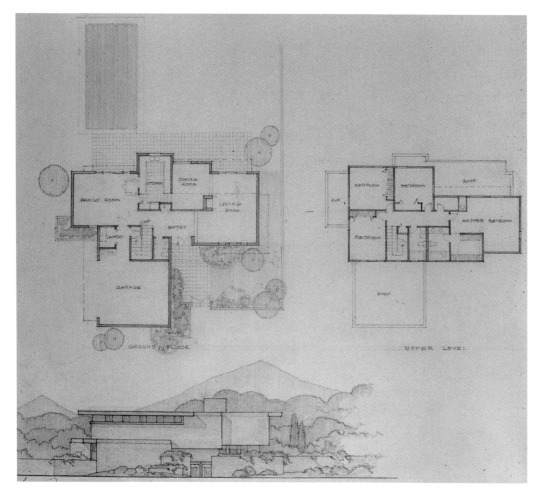

Yet another way to approach a moderate-cost home came with the opportunity to design the 1997 Life Dream House. This is covered in the chapter, "Family Activities."

It is safe to say that one of the most effective ways to substantially reduce the cost of a house is to employ assembly-line technology. The most costly parts of any home, per square foot of space, are kitchens and bathrooms. These areas include expensive appliances, fixtures, cabinets, floor and wall finishes, and a concentration of plumbing and electrical components.

These areas are also quite susceptible to factory assembly, and it is surprising that they are still painstakingly assembled, piece by piece, in the field. Complete kitchens and bathrooms could be made in a factory in a variety of configurations, with options on equipment and finishes. Assembled units could be shipped to a site and incorporated in a home at a much lower cost than the current method, which requires the coordination of many skilled trades.

Virtually no facilities currently exist to do this, but the technology of the automobile and airplane industries has demonstrated our capability. This one step alone could reduce the cost of a home significantly, while increasing quality control.

In our country the chief obstacle to any real solution of the moderate-cost house problem is the fact that our people do not really know how to live. They imagine their idiosyncrasies to be their "tastes," their prejudices to be their predilections, and their ignorance to be virtue — where any beauty of living is concerned.

WHERE TO BUILD

Let your home appear to grow easily from its site and shape it to sympathize with its surroundings. Buildings, too, are children of the earth and sun.

—FLLW

T hree of the great blessings in life are
- to do work that you love and in which you can be most productive;
- to work in the company of people you most like and admire;
- to live in the place that you prefer above all others.

This last consideration is something that I wish a family would think about carefully before determining where to build. Americans have a rather poor record when it comes to "putting down roots." Many families stay in a house only a few years — hardly enough time to get to know the neighbors. We tend to be a nation of house-hoppers. We have many reasons to relocate, such as new job opportunities, a desire for a larger, smaller or better house, better weather, and so forth. In much of the rest of the world, a family lives in the same house for generations.

What is the advantage of putting down some roots? For one thing, if you plan to live in a house for a long time, to raise your family there and to pass it on to your children, you are going to be more concerned about the quality of its design and construction. Certainly more than you would be if you expected to depart in a few years. Many people accept a lower-quality house if they think they will be moving on. Consequently, more and more low-quality houses are built.

Where is the best place to build? The advice that Frank Lloyd Wright gave to his clients was to find a site far out of town. "The city did its work long ago, it is a habit; we do not need it; it is in the way and we could get along very well without it if we were sufficiently intelligent. The

Opposite: *Intelligent people are leaving the city.*

more intelligent people are continually leaving it and those who have not had the experience crowd in where they have been."

"When selecting a site for your house, there is always the question of how close to the city you should be, and that depends on what kind of slave you are. Avoid the suburbs," he admonished, "go way out into the country — what you regard as 'too far.' There is only one solution, one principle, one proceeding which can rid the city of its congestion and that is decentralization.

"Cities are commonly laid out north, south, east, and west. This was just to save the surveyor trouble, I imagine. Anyway, it happened without much thought for the human beings compelled to build homes on those lines and inevitably results in every house having a dark side.

"Since we cannot bring the country into the city, the city must go out into the country. My prescription — first, a good site. Pick a site no one wants, one that has features that give it character — trees, some individuality, perhaps a fault of some kind that exists mostly in the realtor's mind. Then, standing on that site, look about you so that you see what has charm. What is the reason you want to build there? Find out. Then build your house so that you may still look from where you stood upon all that charmed you and lose nothing of what you saw before the house was built but see more."

Living in the city subjects us to air pollution, crowds, noise and crime. Living away from the city, a relationship with nature, open

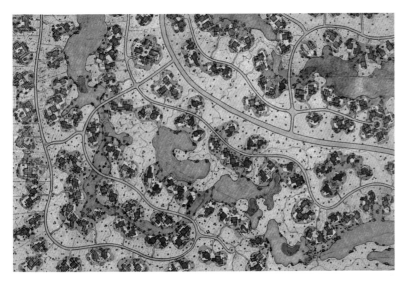

space, fresh air, sunshine and trees becomes possible. The atmosphere is quieter and more relaxed. These gifts of Nature, so easily taken for granted, are free. All we need to do is not abuse them. Land is less expensive in the country than in the city and taxes are lower, so one can afford a larger piece of property.

What is the downside? Lack of fast access to business, services and amenities, shops, schools and airports. Modern technology has overcome some of these concerns. We can conduct business by phone, fax and e-mail. The Internet connects us worldwide.

Small neighborhood centers take care of the bulk of our daily shopping needs. Wright's plan for Broadacre City was based on the idea of decentralization, and much of this is happening today.

In the past, people congregated in cities for several reasons. The primal force was the instinct of mankind to herd together. This may be natural for cattle, but hardly an admirable trait for humans. In the "Dark Ages," most cities had perimeter walls and fortifications that provided security against invasions. Transportation was mostly on foot or horseback, so people wanted to live close to markets, schools and hospitals. Communications before the age of electronics relied on the proximity of people.

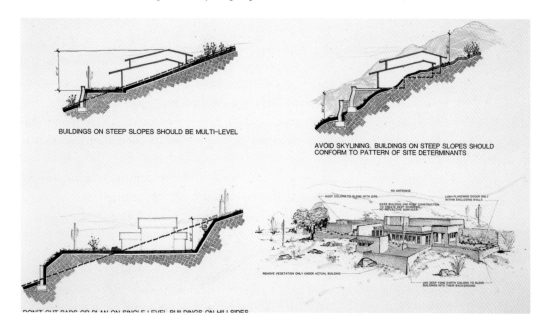

Guidelines for building without destroying the land.

BUILDINGS ON STEEP SLOPES SHOULD BE MULTI-LEVEL

AVOID SKYLINING. BUILDINGS ON STEEP SLOPES SHOULD CONFORM TO PATTERN OF SITE DETERMINANTS

DON'T CUT PADS OR PLAN ON SINGLE LEVEL BUILDINGS ON HILLSIDES

Today we have many methods of transportation and communication that obviate the need to flock together. As more ways are invented to overcome the need for an infrastructure of utilities — such as harnessing and storing solar power, fuel cells and composting human waste, we will have an increased freedom to live away from the city. No matter where we are today, in another city, in another country, or in a moving vehicle, with a cell phone we can be in communication with the rest of the world.

Before deciding whether to live in the suburbs or beyond, I suggest making a list of plus and minus aspects. The minus side might include the time spent in traffic, health concerns from pollution, the constant stress from noise, and the fear of crime and violence. By contrast, living in an open space, breathing fresh air and connecting with Nature refreshes and restores

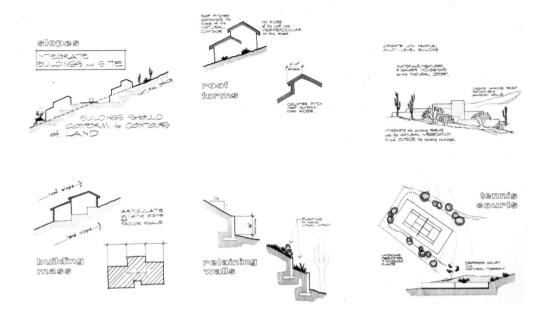

us. It takes some courage to break a tradition, but most people who have escaped the city are grateful for the increase in the quality of their lifestyle.

"Human houses," said Wright, "should not be like boxes, blazing in the sun, nor should we outrage the machine by trying to make dwelling places too complementary to machinery. Any building for humane purposes should be an elemental, sympathetic feature of the ground, complementary to its natural environment, belonging by kinship to the ground."

Typical suburban lots get narrower and narrower. The reason for this is that real estate value is a function of street exposure. The more lots that can be squeezed along a street, the lower the expense per lot for utilities and roads (the infrastructure), and the higher the profits for the developer. A very narrow lot makes it much more challenging, if not almost impossible, to design a beautiful house. When a lot is so tight that a two-car garage takes up more than half its width, the garage becomes the most distinctive design feature of the house. We are all familiar with streets lined on both sides with overhead garage doors. The living part of the home practically vanishes.

It would be wise to consult your architect before you purchase a site. For a family with a moderate budget, the best land is a relatively flat or gently sloping site. If the land slopes less than one percent it will not drain well. A modest slope is preferred, four percent up to ten percent are easy grades. A steeply sloping site, over twenty-five percent, will make construction more expensive. Sloping sites may offer special design opportunities. Sometimes you can find a site that nobody thinks is buildable, so it is offered for a reduced price. In this case a creative architect can often rise to the challenge and come up with a thoughtful design that recognizes opportunities unseen by the real estate agent. If there are empty lots on either side, you will have to remember that your new neighbors may build something quite unexpected that will impact your house.

If your home faces north it should be designed so as to introduce some south light. If it faces east or west you will have to deal with the horizontal rays at sunrise and sunset. If it is located below the level of the sewer line you will have to pump sewage uphill.

What are the weather patterns at your site? From what direction do storms come? Wind, like the other aspects of weather, can be a blessing, but too much can be a curse. Every year, property is subject to storm damage from hurricanes and tornadoes, even strong winds. Damage ranges from a blown-over tree to a blown-away roof.

In hot climates, wind can be funneled so as to create a natural cooling effect. The design of your house and the way it is oriented on your site should take this into account.

Give some consideration to the ability of your site to drain rainwater. In a heavy rain you may have sheet-flow across your property. In the desert area where I live we only get about seven inches of rainfall a year. But every few years we have a storm that floods the streets. We call it a "frog-strangler," and it usually causes a lot of property damage.

Some types of soil are more difficult to build on than others (see "Footings and Foundations"). Another problem to check for is radon, a colorless, odorless gas found in some soils. If it does exist there are ways to keep it out of your house. Some people consider the gas to be beneficial, but this has not been proven. It is generally less costly to build in a temperate climate because footings will not have to be as deep as those subject to frost penetration.

If you are lucky enough to have trees on your land, your architect should try to save them by designing around them. They will also have to be protected during the construction period.

Make every effort to have your power and telephone lines buried underground, otherwise you will be cursed with unsightly poles and wires. They should not be in the same trench as water, gas or sewer.

The floor levels step down in terraces to fit the slope.

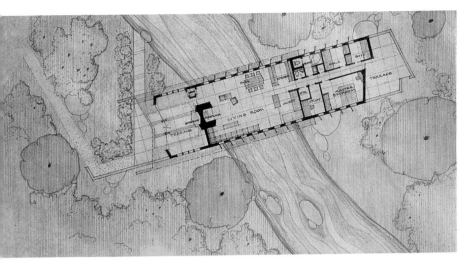

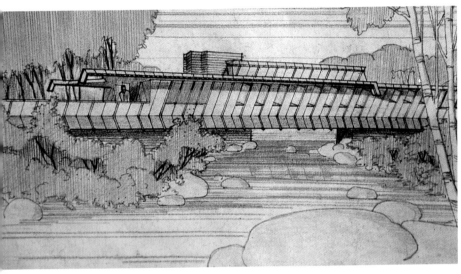

Ideally you would pitch a tent or park an RV on your site and spend a few days there to get the feel of it. If this is impractical, at least spend some time there in the morning and afternoon. Perhaps sit down for a picnic.

How are most sites made ready to go on the market? For years, developers faced with land covered with trees and boulders typically used a bulldozer to remove them. These "obstacles" just make it more difficult to install roads and utilities. On each lot they graded a flat building pad. This approach is starting to change, and many developers now realize that these natural features are priceless assets.

While some cities in the East and Midwest are shrinking, many of those in the Sunbelt are expanding. When Frank Lloyd Wright purchased the land for Taliesin West in 1937 it was only fifty dollars an acre. Over the years, the Phoenix Metropolitan Area has become the sixth largest in the nation. Its density is low, however, with 2,300 people per square mile in contrast to New York, which has 24,000 people per square mile.

The rush to live in the city has been diminishing over the past few decades. In his book, *Megatrends,* John Naisbitt noted that almost half of America now lives in rural areas or small towns. This move is national in scope. It was

Top: A summer cottage that spans a creek.

Above: The walls are built around steel girders salvaged from an old bridge.

triggered by companies that decided to build new facilities where land costs are lower and there is less pollution and crime, where the quality of life is better than in dense urban areas.

You might consider asking an architect's advice on a site before you purchase it. A careful site evaluation will determine both opportunities and constraints. It includes factors such as land costs and economic trends, access, size, shape, topography, drainage, soil type, vegetation, solar orientation, views, weather patterns, wind direction, and existing natural features such as trees, rocks and so forth. The evaluation takes into account the proximity to shops, amenities, and services; the quality of the neighborhood and its growth patterns, adjacent houses, utilities and zoning regulations.

An ancient and traditional Chinese technique called *Feng Shui* was always employed before designing or building anything, whether it was the layout of a city, a building or even a flower arrangement. It is still actively used today to ensure a balance with Nature. Having correct Feng Shui in a home enhances the happiness, tranquility and prosperity of its inhabitants and promotes good *ch'i,* or life force.

Although there is a mystical side to this philosophy, most of its principles are based on good common sense. The literal translation of Feng Shui is "wind and water." The idea is to put the creations of mankind in harmony with the forces of Nature. The optimum design and orientation of a structure is determined by a careful study of the terrain, the hills, rivers and forests, their shapes and positions. The directions of the sun, wind and rain, as well as the other aspects of the natural world, are all taken into account.

The ideas behind organic architecture and Feng Shui are quite close. Both are based on an appreciation for Nature and good common sense.

Heaven is under our feet as well as over our heads.

—Henry David Thoreau

A moderate-cost house in the Virginia woods.

Apprentices learning to

WAYS TO BUILD

In choosing a contractor, the only way to judge him is to look carefully into his previous work. You should be able to tell fairly well, from what he has done, what he may do.

— FLLW

The urge to build is an innate impulse, one that developed as humans evolved. There are many builders to be found in nature. Some instinct guides a beaver to construct a dam, bees to fabricate honeycombs and termites to create a citadel. Nature-built structures are organic in their use of materials and beautiful in their integration of form and function.

When our ancestors evolved from living in caves and moved out into the open, they had no genetic factors to rely on to help them know how to build. They had to invent methods of construction. The environment was hostile; animals and other humans were apt to be enemies. The most permanent structures were fortresses or places of worship.

As humans' sense of beauty, perhaps first ignited as they decorated the walls of their caves, began to grow, it found expression in buildings. The architecture of ancient civilizations is far more than just utilitarian; it is great art. The Sumerians, Persians, Egyptians, Chinese, Japanese, Tibetans, Incas and Mayans all developed an organic architecture, appropriate to its own unique time, place, and culture. But gradually their natural ways were replaced by artificial ways.

The early Greeks first built columns of bundles of wood sticks. When they learned to carve stone, they fluted their stone columns to imitate

Formwork for desert masonry.

the wood bundles. This was the start of classical architecture. The moment stone was carved to look like wood it was a move away from a natural architecture.

In ancient times, designs for structures were made by the builders and the first architects were constructors. As new materials and methods were devised, the design process was separated from the construction operation. This is unfortunate because the two should always work together.

Most homes today are built using the traditional relationship between client, architect and contractor. You, as the owner, engage an architect to prepare a design. Then builders submit bids to build your house. This is a linear approach and is poorly structured because it tends to create adversarial relationships. If you use this method you will probably end up with the lowest bidder, but you may not have the one who will do the best job. Many contractors who bid low make up the difference by charging you for extras. It is scary to realize that almost all of the things built in America, from streets to skyscrapers, are built by the lowest bidders.

Since the builder component (the general contractor and the subcontractors) comes on board after the design is finished and construction documents are completed, they have little input into the design, engineering or building techniques.

It is inefficient to separate the design process from the construction process. Architects should constantly challenge the conventional methods of building and help develop new ideas for construction. Builders should be involved in the design phase to advise on construction techniques.

Sadly, there is little attempt today to devise new ways to construct houses. The vast majority are constructed using the "stick-built" method. The same system is used over and over again. There has to be a simpler and better way to integrate the hundreds of people and processes that are involved in building a house.

First of all there is the client. Then the real estate agent. Probably a bank or finance agency. There are the architect, interior designer and landscape architect. The engineers: civil, structural, plumbing, mechanical and electrical. The consultants: lighting, security, acoustics, audio/video and others. The contractors, the craftsmen who construct your home: carpenters, masons, roofers, painters, and so on. There are the manufacturers and suppliers. Many of them may never know each other but each contributes to the final product, your home.

When you decide to build your home, a prime concern is, "How much will it cost and how can we be sure it will not exceed our budget?" Cost problems, meaning overruns, usually happen because proper controls were not put in place from the start, during the design phase.

In times past, architects were referred to as "master builders." The Greek word *architekton* means master builder. To be regarded as a master builder meant that you had an intimate knowledge of both design and construction. Today, architecture and construction are pretty much separate industries. Just as the architectural profession has, to a large extent, separated those who design residences from those who design commercial, institutional and other types of buildings, so contractors have separated house builders from those that build other types of structures.

The typical procedure for designing and building a custom home is to engage an architect. After you approve a design, construction documents are prepared. Then you ask for competitive bids from several general contractors. If the bids exceed the budget and the owner does not want to increase the budget amount, the design is usually altered, made smaller or simpler, cheaper materials are substituted, and the drawings are sent out to bid again. After you finally obtain a satisfactory bid, you still have to obtain a building permit and then build, furnish and landscape your house. This process is usually frustrating to all parties.

This is the time to check that all switches and outlets are in place.

DESIGN-BUILD

Although currently more applicable to larger construction projects, this could be a more sensible way to build your home. The old-fashioned triad of owner, architect and builder is not the only way to bring your dreams to reality.

Under the design-build process, everybody works together from the start — the architect, engineers, consultants, contractor and the major subcontractors. Ideally, it would include a real estate agent to help you find an appropriate site. The team can integrate site selection, property acquisition, financing,

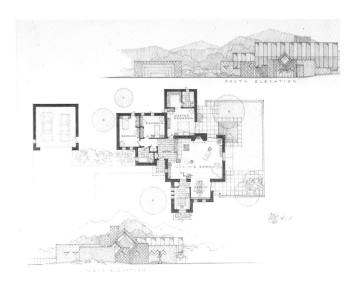

architectural design, interiors and landscaping, lighting, plumbing, climate control, alternative energy and electronic systems. The builder, as a part of the design process, contributes knowledge of building systems and materials. Cost controls are exercised from the outset. Many problems can be avoided if the building part of the team participates in the design phase.

Sometimes people buy a lot and then find out that it has problems they hadn't anticipated, problems that an architect or a civil engineer would have seen.

From the owner's viewpoint, design-build offers the advantage of a single, coordinated source of responsibility for design, cost controls, scheduling, construction and quality assurance.

An integral part of this method is value engineering.

A cast concrete house.

This compares alternative possibilities for materials, construction methods, fixtures and equipment. An analysis of initial costs and long-term costs (maintenance and energy) can effect substantial savings to the owner.

When all participants cooperate, when fixing the problem is the goal, rather than fixing the blame, everybody is a winner. Pointing fingers never solved anything. Cooperation, communication and the coordinated integration of effort are essential to achieving a successful project.

The forms can be reused many times.

The builder may still call for competitive bids from subcontractors who have proven their ability to produce quality work. Design-build is a process you should seriously consider.

Unfortunately, when the process is applied en masse to tract housing (which uses quantity repetition of standard house plans and construction methods), it often results in inferior design and construction. The architect is replaced by a draftsman and the same tired designs are repeated endlessly.

CONSTRUCTION SYSTEMS

The majority of moderate-cost houses are constructed with wood, using the Western or Platform framing method. The walls are two-inch by four-inch studs sheathed with composite plywood. The walls are faced with siding (wood, metal or plastic), or stucco, sometimes a little masonry. Roofs are framed with standard manufactured trusses.

A factory-built "affordable" design.

Much of the integrity of your walls comes from the proper attachment of the sheathing to the studs. A few extra nails are a cheap way to be sure the sheathing is securely attached.

If you use two-inch by six-inch studs instead of two-inch by four-inch you can use thicker insulation. The energy savings will eventually offset the increased lumber cost.

Floors above grade are framed with larger lumber, sized according to the span. Solid blocking or cross bracing must be applied, according to requirements of building codes, to stiffen joists that have longer spans.

Remember that most construction problems occur at joints and connections. Like our own bodies, they are the places most subject to stress and potential failure.

Quality Control

In all likelihood, you know little about construction and probably have no idea whether the carpenters or other workers are taking shortcuts. But check for large knots in joists, and cast your eye along the face of walls to see if they are out of line. You might want to ask a friend to pay a few unexpected visits. Give him a hardhat, a notebook and a camera, and have him walk around the work site. Of course, if he knows what he is doing, so much the better, but his presence alone may be enough to prevent you from being cheated.

You might also engage a construction consultant or a retired builder to do a few inspections for you. Once the framing of your walls and ceilings is covered up, any potential problems are hidden from sight. Taking regular photographs of construction is an excellent idea, especially if you do it before the walls are sheathed. This way you will have a record that may be useful if you want to hang a picture or remodel your home.

Most of us go about building our house in one of three ways:

1. The Manufactured Home. The most cost-effective way of building a single-family detached home is to factory-produce a complete, three-dimensional unit — the so-called mobile home. In truth, it is not really mobile, and seldom travels more than once — from the factory to a mobile home park. The maximum width of a unit, as dictated by highway regulations, is usually twelve feet (fourteen feet in some areas). This method has many advantages

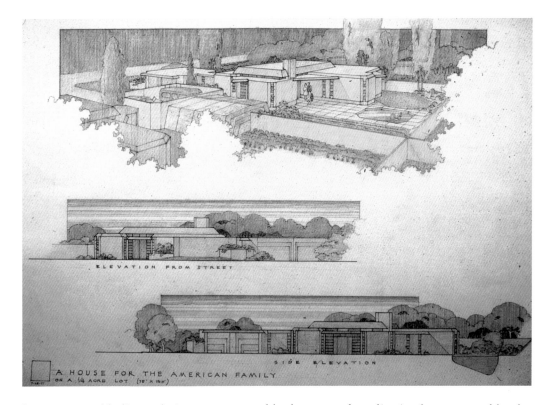

ELEVATION FROM STREET

SIDE ELEVATION

A HOUSE FOR THE AMERICAN FAMILY ON A ¼ ACRE LOT (75' x 150')

because assembly line techniques can control both costs and quality (as demonstrated by the manufacture of automobiles, television sets, and so on). Unfortunately, in the housing industry, factory methods have been assigned almost exclusively to the lowest level of quality.

Mobile homes are usually non-distinctive in design, box-like in shape, poorly made and almost always set on a flat and uninteresting site. They are apt to be crowded together in a park. A "mobile home park" is not much of a park, however, since most of them have almost no open space and only a bare minimum of landscaping.

To economize, manufacturers tend to use both inexpensive materials and unskilled labor. Nevertheless, the assembly line is the most efficient and cost-effective way to build dwelling units. Another way to employ the factory is to manufacture components, such as pre-assembled wall panels, that are shipped to the site and connected together. This method offers more flexibility than mobile homes.

Although the mobile unit is generally looked on with scorn by those who live in "real" houses, it is all many people can afford. The day will come when the benefits of the assembly line will be applied to building houses, particularly in bathrooms and kitchens (the most expensive part of a house to construct). Taliesin Architects contributed in the past to the manufactured home industry through a series of designs for the National Homes Corporation and for Sierra Homes, an Arizona manufacturer.

2. The Portfolio House. Builders, developers, designers and some architects offer a variety of "standard" plans, which are presented in a sales brochure or "portfolio." There may be a half dozen or more models available, and some alternative roof designs are usually offered. The floor plan is sometimes subject to limited modifications, such as adding a room or two. Economies of construction are achieved because the builder has carefully figured and then demonstrated the cost to construct the "Production Home."

The cost of utilities is included in the cost of the lot and all necessary permits have been secured. Costs are reduced because materials are purchased in quantity and subcontractors' prices are lower because of repetition. The same floor plan is used with different exterior style applied — Spanish Colonial, French Provincial, Midwestern, Territorial, California Ranch and so on.

Most of the single-family houses in the United States are built this way. Much attention is paid to making the front façade look impressive, the kitchen is sure to have the latest appliances and bathrooms will have the most recent plumbing fixtures, but the designs look like they were stamped out with a cookie cutter.

However, as long as buyers don't complain, as long as there is a market demand for a product, little will be done to make any significant improvements in design or construction.

Many manufacturers and builders use planned obsolescence. If a product lasts too long, they reason, people will not need to buy a new one. If it is not too well built or is designed in a current style that will look obsolete when styles change, it will need to be replaced.

An organic design, however, is timeless. Over the years it will need to be refurbished, and eventually need new bathroom fixtures and kitchen appliances. The design of the structure, however, will not become outmoded.

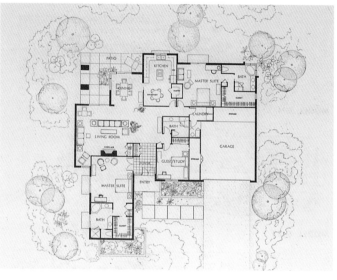

Top: *A ski cabin in New Market, Virginia.*

Above: *Plan for a three-bedroom home.*

3. The "Custom" House. This is a house designed by an architect or designer. In some cases, an owner may design the house and engage a qualified person to prepare the plans. The result of this process is, or should be, a home that exactly fits the needs of a particular person or family. The home is a one-of-a-kind design. Although this is a more expensive method than the ways described above, in the long run it may prove to be more cost-effective. A beautiful and functional home will uplift and energize the members of the family, add quality to everyday life, and continue to appreciate in value for years to come.

Happiness is a very small desk and a very big wastebasket.

—Robert Orben

STYLE AND QUALITY

Fashion is nothing but an induced epidemic.

—George Bernard Shaw

When building a new home, the question many people ask is, "What style do we want?" The problem with selecting a style is that all styles and fashions eventually go out of style. Even the so-called modern style is being replaced by a post-modern style. When this passes from vogue, will we have post-post-modern?

When we live in the United States, where our democratic system of government serves as an ideal for much of the rest of the world, would we want to choose an architectural style that was imported from some other country? Why on earth would we want Spanish Colonial, English Tudor or French Provincial? Why not American?

Opposite: *Integrity is as desirable a quality in a house as it is in a person.*

Left: *Organic architecture is timeless.*

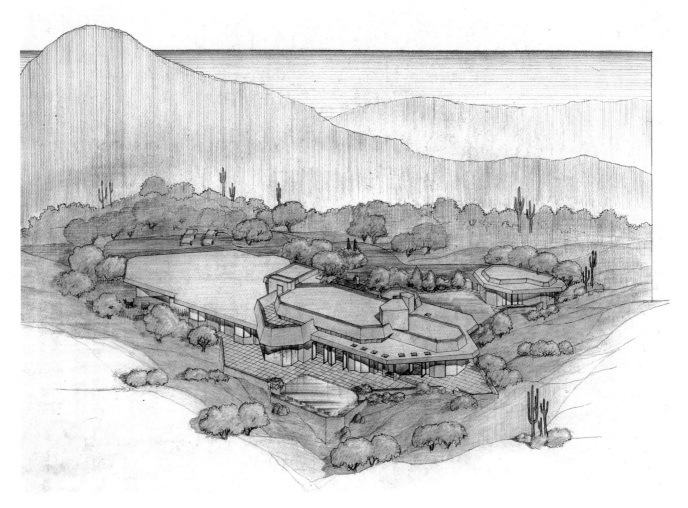

Designs should be based on fundamental principles.

Opposite: *There is no substitute for quality.*

Surely this great country deserves to have its own architecture. There is a significant difference between a style, which means something geographical or historical, and style itself, referring to quality in design. When we say a person has style, we mean character, elegance and grace. A house should have this sort of quality of style, but it doesn't need to be in a current fashion or historic style. Trends come, change and then change again. Let's never confuse a particular style for quality itself. Quality, as we have heard, knows no substitute and has nothing to do with fashions.

Organic architecture goes far beyond what can be classified as a style. It is not classical, modern or contemporary but timeless, always evolving.

What are the qualities that give a home a level of design excellence? I believe that they are largely a matter of common sense. To start with, there should be a lack of pretense. Our home should have integrity. It should manifest a sense of shelter, since that is its prime function. The roof is our home's umbrella. When a roof projects out from an exterior wall it provides shade and casts shadows. Houses without roof overhangs are like a person in the sun or rain, all day, every day, without a hat or umbrella. Shading works most effectively on the south side of your home. It is an effective way to reduce glare as well as heating and cooling demands.

Although you may have to adjust your goals in the choice of materials for your new home

in order to stay within your budget, think hard before you downgrade the quality of the roof over your head.

Your home should have a sense of human scale, and it should not look like some sort of cold, technological machine (unless you plan on living like a robot).

A well-designed house is appropriate to its time, to its location, and to its culture. While advances in technology have improved dramatically and brought major changes to our workplace, our means of transportation and our ways of communicating, they have done little to change and improve the design and function of our home. One-third of all dwellings in the United States were built in the past fifteen years, yet most were designed for the family lifestyle that existed thirty or forty years ago.

America needs a house that provides an environment that enriches life, nurtures the spir-

An enclosed garden court for a house with no space in the rear.

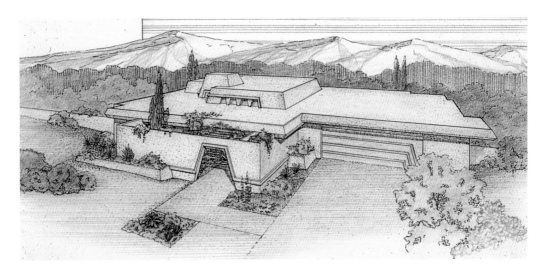

it and inspires creativity. A house to answer the needs and styles of families through all the phases of their lives — as they grow; as their incomes and needs change; as they adapt to the empty nest, with more leisure time and freedom from family responsibilities.

Why do progress and beauty have to be so opposed?

—Anne Morrow Lindbergh

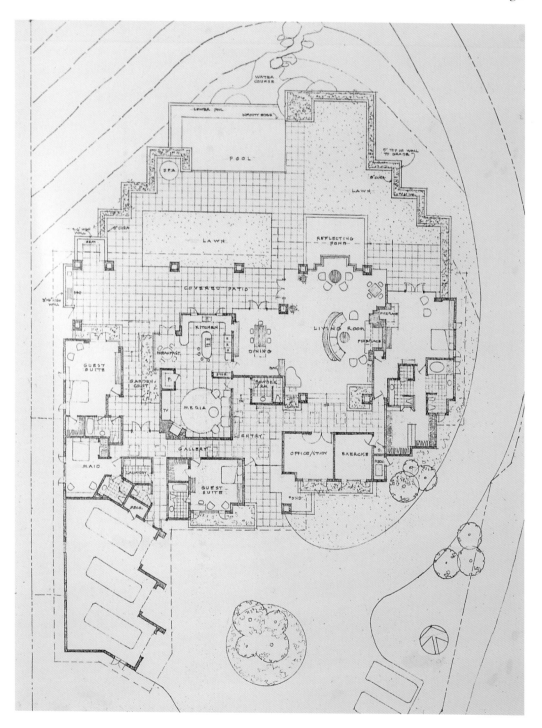

A luxury home for southern California.

*The forms of the boulders on
the site inspired the design.*

DESIGN — LEARNING FROM NATURE

You can't use up creativity. The more you use, the more you have.

—Maya Angelou

Nature is my wellspring of ideas, the teacher for whom I have the greatest reverence. It is probably the only manifestation of our Creator that we will see while we are on this earth. If we want to seek the essence of anything, to truly understand it, be it a creature, a plant, or anything in this universe, we must do more than look at its outer form. We must look

Natural outcropping of limestone.

within. This is a remarkably simple yet very profound idea, developing the ability to look within. Children should learn to develop an "all-seeing eye" while they are quite young. It should be done quite naturally, as a matter of observation rather than scrutiny. But it will cut through veneer and façade.

When you look at a tree, don't just see the beauty of its shape — see beyond the color and texture of its bark, the softness of its leaves, the poetry of its movements in the wind. Sense the principles at work in its design — in its ability to feed from the soil and the air, to utilize the sunlight, to reproduce itself. Appreciate its individuality. Though all trees use similar methods of structure, survival and regeneration, each species is distinct.

The Mabinogion, a collection of Welsh tales dating from the Middle Ages, has an appropriate definition:

Above: *Masonry wall that emulates Nature.*

Right, top: *Igneous rocks in the southwest desert.*

Right, bottom: *Desert masonry made with rocks from the site.*

"An artist is a man with an eye to see Nature, a heart to feel Nature, and the courage to follow Nature."

What can we learn from ancient civilizations and cultures of the past? They can teach us a great deal, especially the Japanese and ancient Mayan. We should not be interested in copying their forms but in identifying what inspired these artists and builders to create beautiful designs. Many lessons can be learned from the simple Japanese print. Underlying this unpretentious art form was a sense of structure.

There are many people who extolled Nature. Walt Whitman, Henry Thoreau, Ralph Waldo Emerson, Louis Sullivan — all were inspired by the beauty and mystery of Nature. Frank Lloyd Wright respected Nature far too much to copy it. In the spiral form of the Guggenheim Museum, for instance, we see the inspiration of the nautilus shell. The building is a good example of an idea emulated rather than imitated. Another example of architecture inspired by Nature is the Asian pagoda, which draws from the pine tree.

Whenever we look to the essential forms that are the mathematical basis for the forms in Nature, and translate them into a geometric abstraction, we have discovered an endless source of design ideas.

We all need inspiration, be it in business, art, science, education or politics. Yet our educational system pays little attention to identifying the sources of inspiration, even though this is the foundation of all creative acts.

The school at Taliesin explores different ways to inspire the apprentices and keep their creative juices flowing. Wright talked to the Fellowship on Sunday mornings. His talks were always impromptu and covered a wide range of subjects, from the movie we saw last night to the state of the nation.

One day he brought in a tray of seashells and set them on the table. He used them to illustrate Nature's housing. Here is an excerpt from that talk:

I wish to give you a little lesson in housing. I will try to show you what "housing" in Nature amounts to. If you really want to study housing, this is the place for it.

Let us turn, carefully, critically, to these beautiful, infinitely varied little creature houses. This is natural housing. Is it on a lower level than ours? In a sense that is true, but is not this humble housing a marvelous manifestation of fertile, organic process? Now where in this bewildering world of organic form is the motive, the impulse, the idea? Here we see that idea. Just one idea in all of them? Yes, but no limitation to variety.

Here are excellent lessons in human housing for young architects. This nature housing is doing exactly the thing that we seem to lack: living in naturally inspired, beautiful forms. See the innate quality of invention in this collection of shells. Each built their house in a beautiful, consistent variation. Each is a matter of natural principle at work on natural design. This multitudinous expression should indicate what design might mean if we were similarly inspired.

There is no good reason why our dwelling-places should be alike all over this country. Why should not our homes be as imaginative in design as these little sea-houses? Why do we need to take any one expression of a formula and carry it out to a dead end?

Here in this collection of little "houses" is one of the most inspiring lessons you could possibly find. Although there is but one generic principle at work and each is doing the same thing to the same end, they are not doing it in the same way. Nature's most beloved asset, individuality, proceeds here and succeeds.

The concordant shapes, varied colors and textures are tributary, obedient to forces exerted from within. Each pattern of ornamentation is appropriate. The exquisite form of each shell is a consequence of innate obedience to forces exerted from within as the shell is formed.

Probably this small being grew in a coral bed, where the shape and every feature of the house was necessary to preserve its life. That is true of all more highly developed, cellular designs. All the "houses" eventually harmonize because of obedience to principle. Here you see what individuality might mean in the architecture of our

Top: *Nature patterns are a source of design inspiration.*

Above: *Each design of Nature is a miracle.*

Above: *Study the principles of Nature.*

Opposite: *The saguaro is an engineering marvel.*

nation if we were similarly inspired by principle. *If you want a lesson in organic structure, wherein what we call ornament is a suitable sequence and consequence of form and method, here it is.*

These natural houses are little poems. Beautiful? Yes, all of them. Some of the creatures seem still young, growing up. Perhaps a new species is being created. When you get to the simple secret governing the inner life and shaping of the sea-shell, when you learn how a common aim persists in its various forms, you will have the secret of characteristic differences in housing that should apply to the human family.

In these internally reinforced shells, structure is shaped by a scarcity of raw materials. Here we see the economical webs of the reinforcing rib instead of a thicker wall-mass. Is each a different idea? No, the idea is generic, but so productive that this infinite variety can go on forever, it is infinite. What is the element in Nature which produces, on principle, such fascinating, rich, harmonious individualities? Is this not the God in them? It is the same element that produces the differences in human beings. What is their secret? This is the major question you should all study as artists. The answer is written in the great book of creation in which you may someday have a page of your own. Because there, in the principles of Nature, is where the artist may find light.

One of the most important lessons we learn from Nature is that the design of everything is based on a mathematical unit system. It applies to the arrangement of atoms in a molecule, to the cellular structure of rocks, plants, and living creatures, even the stars in the heavens.

THE UNIT SYSTEM

Architects must be practical dreamers. A way to keep our feet on the ground is to employ a simple, fundamental geometry to our designs. The unit system is a modular grid, based on the square, rectangle, triangle, hexagon or circle, sometimes a combination of these forms. By using a unit system as the basis of an architectural design, we impose a discipline on our work that organizes it.

In years past, the design of the Japanese house was based on modules that were the size of the tatami sleeping mat. Each room was a multiple of these modules, or units, which determined the size and proportions of the design of the house.

Limitations should be considered an architect's best friends. In Nature we find testimony to the infinite variety of forms that can grow out of the discipline of a unit system. In the plant world, for instance, there is an amazing diversity of form, pattern, texture and color.

Organic architecture can be defined in the phrase, "The part is to the whole as the whole is the part." We can observe this in the sympathetic design relationship between a leaf and the entire tree. Every detail is part of the design theme.

Architecture has been called frozen music. The structure of music is also based on a mathematical unit system. As long as it stays within the mathematics of its system, it is music. Its mathematical basis places no limits on variety in composition. At times we can mix harmony with dissonance. But when the unit system is ignored, the result is noise or cacophony.

Let Nature be your teacher.
—William Wordsworth

FOOTINGS AND FOUNDATIONS

The foundation system of your house is of the utmost importance since it carries the load of the structure down to the ground. The Bible has a parable about the fate of the foolish man who built his house on a poor foundation — it came to an untimely end.

Be sure that you understand the bearing conditions of the soil on your site. Different types of soil have different bearing capacities. For most single-story houses this is not a problem, but it is well worth checking. Soil tests are not costly and could prevent a serious problem. Ask your architect whether a civil or soils engineer should be consulted. If there are other houses nearby there will probably be soils records on file.

In some parts of the country the soil contains clay, which is expansive, meaning it swells when it gets wet. This is a dangerous condition and will require a special type of foundation, such as piers and grade beams. You should avoid building on unsettled ground or organic soils.

All buildings will have some degree of settlement. A well-designed foundation system will have only minimal settlement, and it will be uniform under all parts of your house.

Most clients don't get out to their building site at the time that footings are poured, but your architect should certainly do this. It is an easy way for a less-

A masonry fireplace will need larger footings.

than-honest builder to cheat because he can quickly cover them up with dirt. The local building inspector should inspect and approve all the footings.

Sometimes it is hard to tell if the soil under the footing is undisturbed or properly compacted. Is the reinforcing steel adequate? If your footings start to fail, which may not happen for several years, you may find cracks appearing in your walls and ceilings. In the worst case, a part of your home may collapse.

Good foundations are essential.

A "spread" footing is the most common type for a single-story house on a relatively flat site. The footing should be designed to carry both the "dead load" (the weight of the structure)

and the "live load" (the weight of occupants and contents). For most single story, wood-framed houses this will require a footing that is not less than eight inches deep and sixteen inches wide. If the wall above is masonry, the footing may need to be larger.

It is essential that all footings rest on firm, undisturbed soil. If the bottom of the trench is over-excavated, it should not be filled back with soil, but with concrete. At least two steel reinforcing bars (half-inch diameter or larger) should run continuously through all the footings. There are regulations that establish how the steel bars are located within the concrete and how much they should overlap. The steel bars should not be allowed to sit in the bottom of the footing trench while the concrete is poured but should be raised up so that they end up buried in concrete.

If your site is sloping, the footings will need to be stepped down with the slope. In this case it is important that the steel bars have continuity. In areas where the temperature drops below freezing in the winter, the footings are vulnerable and must extend below the deepest frost penetration line. This frost line varies from region to region. Footings should never be placed on frozen ground because when the soil thaws it will shrink and cause the house to settle.

A well designed foundation has minimal, uniform settlement.

Foundation systems may also need to resist the lateral or uplifting force of wind. A common practice is to set vertical steel anchor bars in the footing that serve to anchor the walls down to the footing. Most building codes will insist on this. Footings must also have adequate drainage. This can be accomplished with a perforated drain tile that is placed in gravel fill and run around the exterior perimeter of the footings. It will need to extend to a point where it can carry water out above grade or into a drywell.

If you have a basement that is below grade the walls will need to resist the horizontal force of ground pressure. This type of wall is called a retaining wall. Placing a layer of gravel or crushed rock against the wall will allow water to be drained away. A perforated drain tile that is set around the outside perimeter of the footings will also serve to carry water away.

If you have a concrete terrace slab that extends out beyond the house (and there is no frost problem) a footing may not be necessary at the outer edge. Instead the edge of the slab may be thickened and reinforced with steel bars.

ROOFS, WATERPROOFING, SKYLIGHTS

Think of the roof as an umbrella against the sun, and then pierce it at reasonable junctures to let shafts of light and sun march across the fluid interior space below.

—FLLW

Your roof fulfills the primary function of your house, which is to shelter you from the elements — sunshine, rain, snow and wind.

In addition, the shape of your roof is likely to be the most significant design feature of your home, the one that defines its architectural character (unless you chose a flat roof that is hidden behind parapets).

As I've stressed before, of all the places to economize in a moderate-cost home, the roof should be at the bottom of the list. It protects your investment. If it is damaged, your possessions are at risk. Although you may have to adjust your choice of building materials to stay within your budget, think hard before you downgrade the quality of the roof over your head.

LEARNING BY EXPERIENCE

One problem architects face is that clients don't enjoy being subjected to experimentation. I certainly never met one who would consider using an untried roofing system. But unless we try out new ideas we cannot expect much progress. Our answer at Taliesin is to experiment on ourselves. When the Fellowship built Taliesin West, the roofs over the office, studio and living room were made out of canvas. The fabric provided a soft and beautiful, evenly distributed light. The material was inexpensive and could be installed quickly, without much skill.

The material was stretched over a wooden frame, much like an oil painting. Each panel was about three feet by seven feet and six inches in size, and the panels were placed between wooden trusses, which were eight feet apart.

Opposite: *The horizontal line is the line of repose.*

The roofs echo the shape
of the evergreen trees.

In a light rain the roof worked well. But in a heavy rain, which might occur only a few times a year, it leaked. Rather than try to seal the joints between the panels and the structural beams with caulking, which would quickly dry out in the Arizona sun, we installed metal gutters underneath to carry out any water that leaked through. It was an "upside down roof."

As time passed, the gutters began to fill with dust. When a heavy rain came, water mixed with the dust to create mud. The mud dried out and formed dams in the gutters. Eventually, water would overflow the gutters and pour down in torrents all over the room.

When I arrived, one of my first jobs was to work on the roofs. Since the canvas roof worked well in good weather, everybody was lulled into a false sense of security. After all, in the desert it only rained for a brief spell and then the sun came out. We just had to remember to put the drawings in the vault.

I spent many weeks on the studio roof and did manage to stay slightly ahead of the curve. As a result of my endeavors I was appointed as the official "roofer" for many years. It was a great opportunity to learn by experience — about the weather, water, the durability of materials, exposure to the sun, expansion and contraction, and so forth. I learned diplomatic ways to deal with those irate people whose desks were located under leaks.

Over the years, we experimented with many different roofing materials. When U.S. Rubber came out with a rubber fabric called Fiberthin, we removed all the canvas (which only lasted a few years in the Arizona sun) and replaced it with this new material. We stretched it tightly over the wooden frames and thought we had at last solved the problem. It allowed a diffused light to enter, and being rubber, would not rot.

Some weeks later we had a real downpour. In a short time the rubber began to stretch and the sags collected puddles. More water just stretched the material even further, until it created great bags of water. From the inside, the ceiling looked like a pod of pregnant whales. We

124

The roof is the most important design element of a house.

had to take garbage bins, set them below the bulges and pierce the rubber with a knife so the water could pour out. We chalked it up to experience. Nothing ventured, nothing gained. The canvas roof returned.

Over the years, we have experimented with all sorts of roofing, caulking and waterproofing materials. We now have relatively trouble-free roofs composed of panels of thermal insulation sandwiched between two layers of thin, rigid plastic. The panels are translucent, so we have the same even, diffused daylight that the canvas supplied.

Over the years we have tried out almost every type of roofing material on the various buildings on the campus. We are still looking for better ones.

ROOF SHAPES

The shape of your roof depends on the configuration of your floor plan, the weather, your budget and the imagination of your architect.

If a roof is strangely shaped or awkward it is probably because the designer made a floor plan without giving much thought to the roof. The idea for the roof probably came later and there was a struggle to make it fit the plan. It is better to incorporate the configuration of the roof as an integral part of the design process, rather than apply something after the floor plan has been worked out.

Both the shape of your roof and the type of roofing that you put on it will depend on the climate in which you live. Do you have snow and ice, rain, high temperatures, lots of sunshine or the possibility of hurricanes or tornadoes? The forces of nature must be considered in the design of a roof and the selection of roofing material. Flat roofs in areas with a lot of snow will put a heavy load on your roof framing. If you have snow, you must consider what happens if it slides off the roof. You don't want it falling in front of your door.

Sloping Roofs

Sloping roofs solve the problem of shedding water better than flat roofs. The most common basic shapes are shed, gable and hip. Less common roofs include gambrel, mansard and butterfly. All of these shapes can be modified and are often combined.

The least expensive roof form is probably the shed roof. Here you get more for your money, you have a more interesting interior space than a flat ceiling, and you get the water off the roof quickly.

Flat Roofs

A flat roof should never be built dead level, but have enough slope to drain water. This can be accomplished by adding furring strips to the top of the joists. Although a roof that pitches one quarter inch per foot will drain, builders seldom construct to such accuracy, so a steeper slope is better.

If you have trees nearby you will have to deal with falling dead leaves that can quickly clog up the roof drains, downspouts and gutters.

Curved Roofs

A curved roof is most easily constructed with curved glu-lam beams. Although concrete is an

Top: *Trellis openings let sunlight cast ever-changing shadow patterns.*

Above: *The shape of the roof trellis openings carry out the design theme.*

ideal material for a curved roof, constructing the formwork is expensive. Other sorts of interesting curvilinear shapes are possible, such as domes and barrel vaults (but probably don't apply to a moderate-cost house).

ROOFING MATERIALS AND METHODS

After the shape or form of your roof is determined, the most appropriate roofing system must be selected. Materials for sloping roofs include shingles of wood, slate, clay tile, ceramic tile, metal or composition. Asphalt shingles are the least expensive but have the least character. A wood shingle roof is lovely but it will have to be reshingled every few years. If you live in an area where there is a fire hazard, be sure to use a fire-retardant variety. To give the roof a distinct look, you can double up the shingles every fifth or sixth course.

A metal roof is more expensive but will last much longer and may be a wise investment. Several types of metal are used, including copper, aluminum, steel and zinc. Copper roofing is durable and beautiful, but costly.

Terne metal is a more affordable product. This is a rust-resistant metal formed by bonding molten terne metal (a zinc and tin alloy) to a base sheet of steel. It originated in Wales in the 1800s.

Metal roofing usually comes in rolls, which require joints to connect the pieces together. The batten or standing seam is recommended because it adds pattern and texture to the roof. Metal shingles are another possibility. "Bermuda"-type roofs have distinct horizontal lines that add character.

For flat roofs there are several types of roofing:

- The built-up membrane, tar and gravel type is available in three-ply, four-ply and five-ply. For this type of roof you can obtain a roofing bond as insurance, but it usually covers only the bare minimum when it comes to repairs, and will not cover damage done by leaks. The major advantage of a bonded roof is that the materials and installation procedure are established by the manufacturer's specifications.
- The modified bitumen roof is composed of a mat of glass or polyester fibers impregnated with a mixture of asphalt and plastic.
- The single-ply membrane "rubber" roof is generally better than a built-up roof and not nearly as messy to apply. It is good at handling expansion and contraction caused by temperature changes.
- Sprayed polyurethane roofing is a liquid that foams, expands and becomes rigid

Top: *Wide roof overhangs shade walls and windows, reducing the heat load.*

Above: *Gable roofs are easily framed with manufactured trusses.*

when it is sprayed on the roof surface. The method is referred to as an F.I.P. system, or "foamed in place." It has some distinct advantages since it eliminates the need for flashing and also adds thermal insulation. It must be coated or it will deteriorate in sunlight. For this reason, the quality of the coating becomes very important. It should not be applied under windy circumstances.

- Liquid applied topcoat systems, which are applied as a protective sealer.

FLASHING

Leaks usually occur not in the roofing material but at the joints. Their weak spots are where one slope meets another (hips and valleys), where a chimney or wall extends above the roof plane, and at skylights. These areas should be "flashed" — covered with a strong, waterproof material as extra protection. You cannot pay too much attention to flashing details, nor be too careful in seeing that they are properly installed. Where the roof meets a chimney, install thruwall flashing that extends clear through to the flue. Generally, membrane roofing and F.I.P. polyurethane can be used for both roofing and flashing.

Left: *The roof soffit and trellis openings are finished in wood.*

Right: *Roof fascia of high-density urathene foam and a patinized copper finish.*

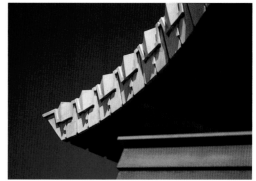

When a roof projects out from an exterior wall it provides shade on the windows and walls below. It also casts shadows, and since these change constantly throughout the day, they make the design of your house more interesting and dynamic.

The edge of a roof terminates in a fascia, which I typically make with sloping wood boards, usually a two-inch by twelve-inch that laps over a smaller board below. To emphasize the rooflines and create interesting shadow patterns, I often design abstract ornaments as an integral part of the roof fascia.

Today there is an affordable technique for creating patterned copper fascias. A full-size section of the roof fascia is built of wood and from this a negative mold is made. A liquid, high-density polyurethane foam is injected into this mold. The foam sets into a solid material.

These fascia pieces are then coated with a metallic copper paint. The copper is treated in the factory with chemicals to create a permanent and beautiful blue-green patina. Almost any shape can be made and the cost is far less than using sheet copper.

WATERPROOFING

There are other parts of your home besides your roof that are subject to water infiltration,

especially walls and floors that are below grade level (grade is the surface of the ground). The type of method you use will depend on whether or not a hydrostatic head (in simple terms, water in the surrounding soil) exists that could exert pressure.

In the construction world, the word "waterproof" is usually replaced by the words "damp-proof" or "weather-tight," since there is a liability issue when a product or process is described as waterproof. Whatever it is called, you want a system that prevents moisture from entering your home.

You need to be especially careful that walls below grade are made watertight before they are backfilled.

Once earth has covered a wall, any remedial treatment is going to be difficult and costly.

Bentonite clay is a natural material that swells when moistened to form an impermeable barrier. It usually comes in the form of corrugated cardboard panels which have their corrugations filled with Bentonite. Other techniques include membranes or fluid applied materials.

Your situation may call for drain tiles around the base of the footings. These tiles will need a place to drain to. If your site has a slope they can drain out on grade at a lower level. They can empty into a storm drain or drywell, but not a sanitary sewer.

Make the roof or ceiling overhead many-leveled and interesting in its intricacy, with high-soaring space contrasted with low, snug alcoves and retreats. Let there be dark, cave-like areas for retreat when your thoughts are dark, and bright, sunny, lofty places for when you are sure and serene.

—FLLW

Top: *A sloping roof will shed water better than a flat one.*

Above: *These ocean-front casitas have sheet metal roofs.*

THERMAL INSULATION

Penny wise, pound foolish.

— Richard Burton

An extremely poor way to save money is by stinting on thermal insulation. Why should you invest in a type of insulation that has a high performance value? Because you will live more comfortably in your home year-round; and in just a few years, you will recover the extra expense of better insulation though reduced utility bills.

The most common type of insulation for the wood-framed house is the fiberglass or mineral wool batt (or blanket) which is stapled between the wall studs and roof joists. The higher its R-value, the better its ability to stop the flow of heat. The temperature indoors often needs to be either higher or lower than it is outdoors, so at times thermal insulation keeps heat in. At other times, it keeps it out.

Air is an excellent insulator, and most thermal insulation works by trapping many tiny pockets of air.

You may remember from high school physics that heat travels in three basic ways: convection (by fluid, usually air or water); by conduction (particle to particle, such as up the handle of your spoon); and by radiation (through electromagnetic energy, such as sunlight). Black or dark surfaces absorb and lose heat faster than white, or shiny surfaces.

I suggest you use at least R-19 batts in the walls and R-30 batts in the roof. If you live in more extreme climates you

Opposite: *A well-insulated roof will reduce your heating and cooling expense.*

Below: *Thermal insulation keeps heat in during winter and out in summer.*

Above: *The cost of insulated glass may be offset by a reduction in utility expenses.*

Right: *The expense of installing superior insulation will soon be recovered.*

should use R-21 insulation in the walls and R-38 in the roof. Be sure to judge the performance of insulation by its R-value, not its thickness. Batt insulation comes with a vapor barrier in the form of metal foil. The most common mistake in installing insulation is to leave gaps. Be sure that the small areas in the framing around doors and windows are all filled.

To give you a perspective of the effectiveness of fiberglass insulation, R-30 batts that are eight-and-a-half inches thick are equivalent to sixty inches of brick.

Loose fill insulation which is poured in is useful as a fill for concrete block but in stud walls tends to settle over time leaving an uninsulated wall at the top. Another insulating method is expanded polyurethane foam. A liquid chemical is injected into the wall cavity. The moment it comes in contact with air it converts into a semi-solid material that has a high insulating value. As it foams up and hardens it fills every crack and crevice. When the foamed-in-place system is used as a roofing material it adds another layer of thermal insulation.

The color of your roof has a lot to do with the amount of heat that comes in from solar radiation. If you live in a predominantly cold climate, you will welcome heat from the sun. If you live in a hot climate, solar heat is undesirable. Ideally, you would be able to change the color of your roof at different times of the day, making it a light color (reflective) on hot, sunny days and a darker color (absorptive) on cold days when you want the sun to help heat your house. Unfortunately, the means to do this are not yet available.

If you live in a hot climate and have a flat roof that is hidden from view, you can paint your roof white or even silver to reflect heat.

Progress is not an accident, but a necessity . . . It is part of nature.

—Herbert Spencer

A well-insulated roof will reduce your heating and cooling expense.

133

MATERIALS, COLORS, TEXTURES

Bring out the nature of the materials, let their nature intimately into your scheme.

—FLLW

Sometimes building materials are used with little regard for their individual characteristics, their essential nature. At the time of the Industrial Revolution, materials were often considered by architects to be just "grist for the mill." Machines were busy stamping out patterns, casting forms, and turning materials on lathes, and it didn't much matter whether it was wood, metal, cement, clay or plaster.

The ancient builders seemed to appreciate something about the nature of materials. Most of the ancient buildings of past civilizations were made of stone. The Gothic cathedrals, Mayan temples and Egyptian pyramids all show an understanding of the nature of stone. In the masonry walls of temples in South America, stones were cut so precisely that even today a knife blade cannot be inserted in the joints. The stones were ingeniously cut in interlocking jigsaw patterns and have survived many major earthquakes without damage.

In the Far East, builders in medieval times were also sensitive to the nature of different materials and used them with deep respect for their unique and distinctive qualities.

When you or your architect are designing a house you should understand something about the nature and unique characteristics that distinguish

Opposite: *Stone may be more affordable if applied as a veneer.*

Below: *Respect the unique qualities of each building material.*

Materials for a home should be "high touch" rather than "high-tech."

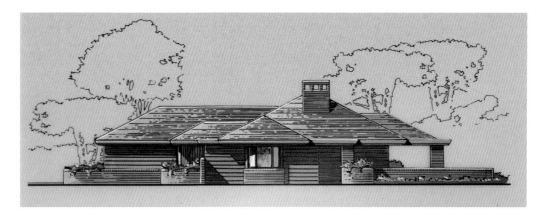

Use earth-tone colored materials to blend with the landscape.

the different types of building material. When you use a material with a true appreciation for its special qualities, the result will look natural and appropriate. There are several factors to consider when selecting a material — strength, durability, workability, weight, hardness, color and texture; and, of course, costs and availability.

A visit to a house that is designed according to organic principles will show you its sensitivity to the nature of materials. Everything is kept as simple as possible. You will not find a large number of different materials. Perhaps a concrete floor, masonry and wood walls, glass doors and windows in wood frames. You won't find one material masquerading as another.

Over the past century, three new materials revolutionized architecture — concrete, steel and glass.

REINFORCED CONCRETE

Desert masonry — concrete with rocks found on the site.

Reinforced concrete combines two different materials — concrete, which is strong in compression, and steel, which is strong in tension. The combination produces a material that resists both compressive and tensile forces.

Portland cement, aggregate (sand and gravel) and water are mixed at a batching plant and delivered to the site by a ready-mix truck. Before the concrete sets up it can be cast or molded into different shapes. Steel, in the form of rods or metal mesh, is placed in the form before the concrete is poured.

The Biblical advice to build a good foundation under your house still holds true. The base for your walls will be footings of reinforced concrete. These should be inspected and approved by the local building inspector before they are covered with earth. In climates where it freezes in the winter, the bottom of footings must be below the frost line (the building inspection department has this information).

If your site has a significant slope you may need to build a retaining wall. This will require engineering. If the earth behind the wall gets wet it can exert great pressure, so the wall must have adequate steel reinforcing. It should also have a gravel backfill and possibly drain tiles to drain out the water.

A concrete floor with integral color.

137

The stone walls of your home will last for generations.

Concrete is an ideal material for the ground level floor of your house. It is durable, fire- and termite-proof, does not rot and is relatively inexpensive. It is, however, subject to cracking if not cured properly while it hardens. The curing process takes several weeks. During this period the slab should be kept moist. This is usually done by covering it with a plastic sheet. Cracks may also occur later if a slab-on-grade does not rest on properly compacted fill.

Parts of the U. S. are plagued with termites. They exist in the soil below or near your house and find their way up through cracks or inside "mud" tunnels that they manufacture. In their search for wood to eat, they can chew through plastic and foam insulation. To control them, the soil is usually chemically treated before a slab is poured. A better, non-toxic way to deal with termites is to place a four-inch-thick layer of sand beneath slabs and foundations and outside stem walls. In Hawaii, these are known as basaltic termite barriers. Other methods include metal shields and termite mesh.

A monolithic concrete floor with a smooth (hard-troweled) finish is relatively inexpensive and lasts a long time. A galvanized metal wire mesh is laid before the slab is poured and embedded in the concrete, which reduces the potential for cracks.

The surface can be finished in a variety of colors. There are two ways to achieve this. Colored powder can be added to ready-mix concrete in the delivery truck, or it can be dusted on the surface of the wet concrete slab and troweled in during the finishing process. The dust-on method provides the best surface, but does require skill on the part of the cement finishers. I like to use rust or tile red color.

The concrete slab is a way to visually express the basic "unit system" on which the house was designed. The unit or grid lines can be either scored with a trowel in the wet concrete, or cut in with a machine saw after the concrete had cured. The pattern in the floor showed how each part of the design is related to a central geometric theme.

Constructing an integrally colored slab with scored unit lines requires some skill and the process is intolerant of mistakes. Extreme heat or freezing weather also affects the process. Once in place, it provides a beautiful, long-lasting, cost-effective floor that can be waxed and polished and is easy to maintain.

There are additives and curing methods that increase the workability, strength and durability of concrete, but to obtain a quality finish still requires human skill.

MASONRY — STONE, BRICK AND CONCRETE BLOCK

These materials are solid and durable, strong in resisting compression. They will sustain heavy vertical loads, but like concrete, need to be reinforced with steel if they are to resist tensile forces. To avoid the need for steel, masonry units can be formed into arches or domes, shapes that transfer vertical loads to the side and keep the units constantly squeezed together.

The inherent characteristic of masonry is one of massiveness, a quality that should be expressed in the way it is used in a design.

I recommend using only one type of masonry material in a house. Don't mix stone with brick or concrete block. Keep it simple. Use the same type of masonry on the inside as outside. Your house will have more integrity. You should, however, use firebrick on the back wall of a fireplace that burns wood or coal.

If you have stone or brick walls you can use concrete block as a backup, also for walls and in basements and areas that are hidden from view.

Frank Lloyd Wright's own home at Taliesin in Wisconsin is a good example of an appropriate way to use masonry. The limestone walls are made with long, thin stones. Some of these stones project out from the face of the wall, emulating the way the material appears in its natural state in a quarry.

The good way to lay up stone is to use the "ashlar pattern." This can be "uncoursed ledge rock" (which is my recommendation), "random broken coursed" or "random coursed."

At Taliesin West, the local stone is of the igneous variety and much harder. It cannot be split. Wright invented a technique for "desert masonry" walls that is suitable to the shapes and nature of the rocks.

Wood forms are constructed and rocks are placed inside, their best face up against the form. Then a dry mix of concrete is tamped into the form. After the concrete has set the form is stripped off. This method is inexpensive as far as materials are concerned but costly because it is labor-intensive.

A more affordable type of stone is one that is manufactured out of concrete. Called faux stone, it imitates natural stone and comes in a wide variety of textures and colors. Faux stone is used as a veneer and backed up with concrete block.

Top: *Roman brick is used in the walls, terraces and steps.*

Center: *Mortar is colored to match the brick.*

Bottom: *Concrete block with flush vertical joints and raked horizontal joints.*

When I use brick or concrete block (also known as CMU — concrete masonry units), I call for the horizontal joints to be raked half an inch deep and the vertical joints to be struck flush. This simple technique adds to the texture of the wall and creates a sense of horizontality.

For brick walls I recommend coloring the grout to match the color of the brick.

WOOD

Most moderate-cost homes in America are framed in wood, although light steel framing is becoming more affordable in some parts of the country and has some advantages.

The ability of wood to endure on the exterior of a building depends on the climate. Its enemies are water, sunlight and termites. Water can cause swelling, then shrinkage, splitting, and rotting. The sun also causes wood to swell, shrink and fade in color.

Opposite: Curved walls are easy to build with masonry.

Wood is the most humanly intimate of all building materials. For many years houses in America were ornamented with a great abundance of decoration, much of it in the form of woodcarvings. This sort of fussy ornament caused an enormous waste of material, since most of the wood ended up as shavings and sawdust on the factory floor. Detailing of wood trim should be kept simple. We should rely more on the natural beauty of wood grain and less on the use of intricate carved shapes.

Use just one species of wood on the exterior and one on the interior. Don't mix three or four different species in the same house.

On the exterior of a house, wood walls can be simple plain boards and battens. These are usually set horizontally or vertically, sometimes diagonally.

Wood shingles of cedar (red or white) or redwood can be used for both roofs and walls. To make them more interesting, consider using thick butt shingles and doubling up every fourth or fifth course.

Plywood is useful both as a structural material and interior finish. Structurally, it is more economical than solid lumber. Plywood is strong and if not too thick it can be curved, in which case it becomes even stronger (during the Second World War it was used to make Mosquito Bombers and PT boats). It can be cut to show a variety of grain patterns — plain sliced, rift or rotary cut.

Above left: Wood is the warmest and most sympathetic building material.

Above right: A clear finish reveals the natural beauty of wood.

*Lapped redwood boards
used for both the exterior
and interior.*

Since the exposed veneer of plywood is very thin, it is a more economical way to use expensive hardwoods than solid lumber. For interior use, hardwood veneer plywood is available in many species of wood. I prefer oak or mahogany. Cherry and teak are beautiful but more costly. I seldom use maple or birch because they have less character in grain and color.

Plywood comes in a variety of qualities and grain configurations. Rotary cut is the least expensive but usually the least attractive. Rift cut, flat and quarter sliced are more refined.

As for doors, I prefer the flush-surface type to paneled type. If you use "French" doors (glazed wood doors) I recommend simple wood frames with plain glass and no muntins (the small bars or moldings that separate panes of glass in a multipane door or window).

Until the wood has a clear sealer applied, the quality of the grain cannot be appreciated. Whenever possible, wood should have a clear matte finish that allows the natural beauty of the grain and color to be seen. I seldom allow wood on the interior to be painted. Wood table and counter tops should get a gloss finish.

When wood is painted, the grain is obscured. There is no substitute for the natural beauty of its subtle grain and color variations. In more temperate climates, a natural exterior finish will last much longer, and there are some good clear finishes available. I use a natural wood finish made by Sikkens.

There are some excellent translucent finishes available today that are quite durable, including polyurethanes for the interior, and an oil and alkyd resin product by Sikkens for exterior surfaces.

GLASS
Of all "modern" materials that serve us, glass might be said to have had the most significant impact. It brought us the telescope, and this expanded our world out to the cosmos.

It also made the microscope possible, which led to the discovery of a universe inside our perceptible world. Glass brought daylight into our buildings, while keeping the weather out, and allowed the inhabitants to see outside. Can you imagine what life was like without it?

Glass is about three-quarters silica sand mixed with some soda and lime. Its history extends back to the time of the ancient Sumerians, who used it primarily for jewelry and drinking vessels. Up until the nineteenth century it came only in small pieces or panes. The invention of plate glass, which could be made in much larger and stronger pieces, gave new possibilities to architecture that were almost unthinkable before. Most glass today is "float glass," a process developed by Alastair Pilkington in the fifties.

Frank Lloyd Wright called glass "the most precious of the architect's new super-materials":

> It amounts to a new qualification of life itself. The nature of glass is to provide an
> invisible barrier, air in air to keep air out or keep it in. By means of glass, open
> reaches of the ground may enter into a building and interior space may reach out
> and associate with exterior space. The ground and the building will thus become
> more and more obviously directly related to each other in openness and intimacy;
> not only as environment but also as a good pattern for life within the building. It is
> by way of glass that the sunlit space becomes the most useful servant of a higher

Mitered glass at the corners helps "destroy the box."

order of the human spirit. Integral character is gained when extended vistas marry
buildings with ground levels or blend them with slopes and gardens.

When Wright left Adler and Sullivan in 1893 and opened up an independent office, he installed a plate glass door at the entrance, one of the first of its kind. He had many imaginative ideas for glass. When he wanted to partially obscure a view, such as between a house and cars on the street, he used art glass patterns. In the Johnson Wax Building he used Pyrex glass tubes which obscure view but transmit a diffused light. He "floated" the dome of the Greek Orthodox Church on glass balls. The entire roof the Beth Sholom Synagogue is made of translucent corrugated wireglass. By day it is a shimmering symbol of Mount Sinai. By night it is a pyramid of light.

"Imagine a city," Wright said, "iridescent by day, luminous by night, imperishable! Buildings, shimmering fabrics, woven of rich glass; glass all clear or part opaque and part clear, patterned in color or stamped to harmonize with the metal tracery that holds it all together."

Glass can be used for insulation. A characteristic of the material is that while it is molten it is ductile and can be drawn out and spun into thin fibers. The fibers can then be spun together to make a blanket, which we know as fiberglass batt insulation.

In the forties Wright's design for the Rogers Lacy Hotel to be built in Dallas was clad with translucent glazing panels in diamond-shaped patterns. The panels, or light-screens, were composed of glass wool sandwiched between two panes of glass. The building was never constructed, but would have been beautiful, providing a diffused glow of light to the interior during the day and radiating a soft light to the city at night. Each panel overlapped the one below so that rainwater would drip clear and not stain the building.

I have never liked the double-hung window, which slides up and down vertically like a guillotine. Instead, I use side-hinged casement windows and "French" doors which open out.

The mitered glass corner is a design technique that clearly helps "destroy the box" in architecture. The method we use today is called a "butt miter." One sheet of glass laps the other and clear silicone holds them together. The edges of the glass panels are "seamed" at the glass shop before installation.

An obvious concern about using large areas of glass is that it has much lower insulative qualities than the wood or masonry walls of your house. Besides bringing in light, it conducts heat and cold. For this reason you should consider using double-glazing. Sunlight also includes ultraviolet (UV) rays, which, besides fading drapery, carpets and furniture, are hard on our eyesight. Tinted glass helps alleviate this problem.

There are several basic design considerations. When you are laying out the floor plan of your home, bear in mind the path of the sun and its changing angles throughout the day and seasons of the year. There are many ways to control sunlight and use it to a good advantage. The plan should be oriented to the best advantage. Thought should be given to the location of rooms vis-à-vis the path of the sun. Roof overhangs, trellises and clerestory windows are useful devices, as are awnings, screens, blinds and drapery.

A good solution to sun protection is provided by roll-up screens of fiberglass fabric. They allow a clear view out but screen out eighty to ninety percent of the sun's heat and glare. They are mounted above the window, either on the exterior or interior, and are operated either manually or by electric motors (which can be controlled automatically by a photocell).

Don't forget that well-placed trees and shrubs will do their share.

As for glass itself, there are on the market many types of "intelligent" or "smart" glass. Glass can be tinted gray, bronze or green. I like the green tint since it blends well with the color of the trees and shrubs in your garden. Low-E glass, which stands for low emissivity, should be used whenever possible. The best, in my estimation, is green tint, double-glazed, low-E glass. It has a performance rating of 1.36, about the highest of all the glazing types. If you are using butt-mitered corners, you will have to revert to single glazing at the corner (but with the same tint).

In the future our houses may have photochromic glass. Currently used for sunglasses and the solar cells of space capsules, it automatically darkens when exposed to more light.

Another new product is photo-catalytic glass, which is self-cleaning (on the outside face). It has a metal oxide coating that interacts with the sun's rays to break down and dissolve dirt.

You will need to use safety glazing in certain areas (as specified by building codes). This includes glass doors, railings, shower and tub enclosures and skylights. The types are laminated, tempered and wired glass. The maximum size of glass may be limited by the wind characteristics in your area. Glazing companies can supply that information.

One of the earliest applications of glass was in cathedral windows. Chemicals were added to the molten mix to create various colors. The pieces of glass in the windows were chunks, rather than panes, and were held together with lead to form beautiful art glass patterns. Since many of Wright's houses were on city lots, he used colored glass in abstract patterns to partially obscure the view of other houses and street traffic. The design of the windows was different for each house and the patterns expressed variations of the basic geometry of the building. He even discovered a special way to build them that was far superior to the system of lead came and soldered joints, the traditional way to keep stained glass pieces in place.

Pieces of colored glass were laid in a flat container and copper wires run between each piece. A liquid containing copper in suspension was poured over the glass. An electric current

Green-tinted, low-emissivity glass cuts down on glare and energy costs.

was run through the wires. Through the process of electrolysis, the wires attracted more copper from the solution until they grew larger and built up a bead that extended over the edge of the glass. The process was called electro-glazing. It produced a delicate, yet strong, integral copper frame that held all the pieces of glass in place. These windows today are considered to be art treasures. The process seems to have been lost after the person who invented it died, and later art glass windows were made with zinc came coated with copper or brass. A favorite technique in the manufacture of art glass is luster coating. Metallic chemicals are sprayed on the molten glass to create an iridescent rainbow-colored glaze. There is also opalescent glass and flashed glass, which come in various colors and textures.

When I was an apprentice at Taliesin I started designing and constructing art glass windows, skylights and tables, including some for Mr. and Mrs. Wright. Although I no longer do the manufacturing part, I still continue to design art glass for many of my houses and buildings.

PLASTIC

Plastic is the "new kid on the block" when it comes to building materials. Although the industry is growing at a high speed, its application in residential architecture is disappointing. While we see a wide range of products — from vapor barriers and coatings for electrical wire to laminated countertops and toilet seats — plastic is still regarded as being best suited to the manufacture of disposable products. In architecture we expect materials to be cost effective, good looking and long lasting.

Many building materials, such as stone, concrete and ceramic tile, are quite durable. Softer materials, such as wood and plaster, can be refinished after they show signs of wear. Some types of plastic, however, have a shorter lifespan, especially when exposed to sunlight. A thin plastic sheet, such as a vapor barrier of polyethylene, must be kept covered, as it deteriorates rapidly in sunlight. When plastic is used as an architectural finish, there is another problem: if the surface is damaged, it is difficult to restore its original appearance.

In acrylic or polycarbonate form plastic works well for skylights. Plastic siding, roof tiles and roof shakes work satisfactorily but tend to look cheap. In PVC form, plastic works fairly well for plumbing (as long as pipes are not exposed to sunlight or physical movement). The old problems associated with plastic piping, such as brittleness, supposedly have been solved but this needs to be proven over time.

Plastic laminate (Formica, Micarta and so on) comes in a wide variety of colors. You can create good-looking, durable, easy-to-clean countertops for kitchens and bathrooms with this material. I recommend a solid color (such as a tile or rust red). If you inlay the plastic laminate top and run a wood nosing around the edge, you can achieve a quality look at a cost far below ceramic tile. My preference is a one-and-a-half-inch half-round hardwood (oak or mahogany) nosing.

A more expensive but highly effective product for countertops is Corian. Corian nosings can be specified to have wood inlays.

Plastic is a poor substitute for glass, since it is far more expensive and much less durable. As a powder coating for architectural metalwork it is no better than paint, fading in sunlight and being hard to recoat. Melamine coatings (on kitchen cabinets for instance), once scratched or chipped, are almost impossible to retouch. A bad feature of plastic is that it quickly generates noxious fumes in a fire.

Plastic should not try to imitate other materials, an easy route to take with a material that can be cast or molded to almost any shape, colored and textured to almost any pattern. When it tries to imitate wood grain the result is cheap, an insult to the natural beauty of wood.

Plastic is already replacing many component parts in appliances, fixtures, equipment and hardware that were formerly made with metal. In the future we can expect the application of plastics in architecture to develop far beyond its current uses.

STUCCO AND DRYWALL

Many exterior walls and soffits (the surface below roof overhangs) are made of stucco (the name for exterior plaster). To withstand weather, stucco is made with Portland cement. It comes in a variety of premixed colors and is usually applied over paper-backed metal lath. Since it is subject to cracking, it is important to install control and expansion joints at regular intervals. An exterior grade of drywall is also available.

If you have overhanging eaves you must provide vents in the soffit. This allows the air

The texture is raked in with a comb before the stucco sets up.

within the structural framing to breathe. The best type of soffit vent is a continuous metal type, installed next to the roof fascia.

Stucco is being replaced by Exterior Insulation Finish Systems (EIFS), Dryvit being one of the best known. A layer of rigid insulation board is applied to the structure, fiberglass mesh attached, and a thin coating of "plasticized" stucco is troweled over. The advantage of this system is that it places the insulating layer where it belongs, on the exterior face of the wall. For this reason it is sometimes called "outsulation." The technique virtually eliminates the possibility of cracks occurring.

Virtually all interior walls and ceilings today are made with drywall (gypsum wallboard). Drywall has replaced the messy process of plastering, although surfaces with compound curves are still made with troweled-on gypsum plaster. In bathrooms, kitchens and other wet areas use moisture-resistant drywall.

A variety of textures are available in both stucco and drywall. I recommend a sand float finish. This can be achieved several ways, but the result should look as even as possible — something like a sheet of medium-grit sandpaper. For the walls of the Myers house in Scottsdale I created a new texture using a sheet metal comb with teeth spaced about an inch apart. The wet stucco was raked vertically to create fine vertical lines.

Top: *The gray cement plaster is left unpainted.*

Above: *The exterior insulation finish system (EIFS) overcomes the problem of cracks.*

METALS

In 1856 the Bessemer process was invented. The world now had an inexpensive way to produce steel. The amazing tensile strength of steel was demonstrated by the engineer John A. Roebling in the construction of the world's first suspension bridge — the Brooklyn Bridge. Spanning 1,600 feet, it was heralded as the eighth wonder of the world.

Steel had an enormous impact on architecture, both as framing members (columns, girders and beams), and as a component of reinforced concrete. Steel allowed architects to cantilever roofs and balconies out into space, creating innovative architectural ideas that could hardly have been imagined before.

Another useful metal is aluminum, a product of the nineteenth century. This metal, and its various alloys, is very strong and light in weight. It comes in sheet or wire form and can be cast into shapes.

Copper is a beautiful metal, a good choice for roofing, flashing and patterned fascias. It used to take years to develop a green-blue patina. Today we need not wait; the process can be instantaneous and permanent with the application of chemicals (such as Frazee's Copper Patina Package). Metal roofs, properly installed with allowances for expansion and contraction, will last a long time.

A good use of metal in residences is in manufactured windows. Window sash is available with metal or vinyl cladding over wood, which precludes the problems that wood has when exposed to weather. Metal surfaces are generally more appropriate to buildings than residences, but there are some beautiful etched-metal finishes, applicable for table, desk and countertops.

ROOF TILES

Clay or concrete roof tiles come in Spanish Mission style and also as a flat, interlocking type. A tile roof is durable as long as nobody tries to walk on it. It should have a minimum pitch of four inches in twelve inches. Spanish tiles look more appropriate in the Southwest and California than other parts of the country.

Slate, a natural stone, is used more in Europe than America, and slate tile roofs have lasted for centuries.

Tile roofs are durable but they are heavy — the roof framing will need to be stronger.

CERAMIC TILE, MARBLE AND GRANITE

These materials are used primarily for floors, walls and countertops. Ceramic tile is a more reasonable choice than marble or granite, which are inappropriate in a moderate-cost house — except in smaller quantities. Select less expensive materials that are simple, good-looking, durable and easy to clean. If you visit showrooms that display these products, you may be overwhelmed by the variety of types available. They range from simple monotone ceramic tiles to exotic quarried stones. Some are domestic, some imported, and they come in all sorts of shapes, sizes and colors.

A quarry tile floor is a possibility you might consider for your entry space, kitchen and bathrooms. The tiles come in orange and buff tones.

Decorators often like to use a different tile in each bathroom. Why not use the same tile? It will be less expensive and there will be less waste. I like one-inch by one-inch unglazed mosaic tiles for both kitchens and bathrooms. These small tiles are laid in sheets and have the advantage of fitting easily around curved surfaces. Floor tiles must be the unglazed type because glazed tiles are slippery when wet.

I recommend you use grout that is integrally colored to match the tile. If you don't request this you will get white grout which will highlight any uneven joints. After installation, a clear sealer should be applied.

COLOR AND TEXTURE

Nature provides the best palette for architecture. Color is much richer when it has some texture. I recommend warm and optimistic earth tones rather than cold pastel colors. Buff, cream, parchment or ivory is preferred over pure white. You can find perfect color schemes in the forest, the mountains or the desert. Don't forget about the colors of earth, sand, rocks or dead leaves.

I believe a blade of grass is no less than the journeywork of the stars.

– Walt Whitman

THE AUTOMOBILE

It goes without saying that you should never have more children than you have car windows.
—Erma Bombeck

When I first knew Mr. Wright he had a beautiful twelve-cylinder 1951 Lincoln Continental. He had modified it into a cabriolet style, replacing the rear part of the top with a rounded metal roof and making the driver's compartment convertible. The bubble-top shape was formed with lead, so the car was quite heavy. The roof over the front seat was a convertible top made of leather. The windshield was chopped down so it was only about fourteen inches high. There was no rear window in the bubble-top, only small half-moon windows on the sides. When he sat in the back with a fur robe on his lap he rode in complete privacy. His daughter, Iovanna, referred to it irreverently as "Daddy's Love Wagon."

Mrs. Wright had her own Lincoln Continental. Like the cabriolet, it was painted Cherokee Red. The senior apprentices each had a sporty two-door Crosley convertible. All the vehicles at Taliesin — the cars, dump truck, pickup, stake truck and van — were painted Cherokee Red.

Wes Peters had a Duesenberg supercharged model J convertible. Then he got a Mercedes Gullwing 300-SL. It would easily outrun the police, so whenever it zipped by they soon gave up the chase and called for a roadblock ahead. I made a trip

Opposite: *Mr. Wright's Lincoln cabriolet.*

Below: *Mr. & Mrs. Wright in their Acedes.*

Top: *A side-entry garage.*

Above: *A detached garage.*

to Wisconsin with Wes in this incredible car and we spent as much time in court as on the road. He let me use it when I spent summers in Arizona supervising the construction of the Gammage Auditorium. Other exotic cars at Taliesin included a Pierce Arrow, Jaguar, Cord, Acedes, Riley and an MG.

About the time I arrived, Mr. Wright had stopped driving and would give Mrs. Wright or one of the apprentices that task. Eventually the task fell to Dick Carney, but I did have the opportunity to drive him a few times.

I had a harrowing experience when I was asked to drive the Lincoln cabriolet back to Taliesin from the garage in Madison. When I came up to the first stop sign and applied the brakes, nothing happened. The car sailed right on through the intersection. I proceeded on carefully and was later informed that the brakes were mechanical, not hydraulic. Even worse, a device had been installed to save gasoline. A small lever under the dashboard would disengage the motor from the drivetrain so that the car was freewheeling. Coasting may have saved gas but with such a heavy car it was living on the edge.

Mr. Wright actually designed an automobile. He worked with my father-in-law, Heinrich Schneider, inventor of the hydromatic drive, to create a three-wheeled "road machine." It never went into production though — it was too far ahead of its time. His book, *The Living City*, includes sketches of the design. It had some unusual features. It sat three people abreast, with the driver in the center, steering with a tiller. The motor turned two six-foot-diameter drive wheels. Because Wright intended the car to travel at speeds well over a hundred miles an hour, he used large wheels to keep the rim speed low. The larger the circumference, the slower the speed of the tire as it meets the ground.

Although he knew little about the computer, which was in its infancy in the fifties, Wright anticipated it and planned for cars to be controlled by a universal highway communication system. A driver would enter the vehicle and simply state a destination. The car would start up and drive without human assistance. It would automatically navigate the streets to get there. Street

Below: A carport extends the roof and adds to the "sense of shelter."

Bottom: A detached, side-entry garage.

lighting was built into the road curbs, together with electronic signal devices that adjusted the speed and spacing of all vehicles. With all human error removed, there would be virtually no accidents. Cars could travel safely at much higher speeds.

Several of us helped prepare the drawings of his ideas for Broadacre City (which he was then calling The Living City). I made two sketches, one showing the road machine and the other a five-seat helicopter. This was an aircraft that was also guided by electronic beams, programmed to respond to a command such as, "Take us to see Aunt Nellie." As the passengers relaxed, the machine flew to this destination on full automatic pilot. When it arrived,

A front-entry garage.   the rotor blades folded up and its single support leg fitted into a socket on the ground where the electric motor was recharged. I also sketched in some atomic boats and barges.

It is hard to overstate the impact of the automobile. In only three generations, it has totally changed the way we travel, the way we work and the way we live. Cars have become so essential to us that they often get top priority, whether we are planning a house or a city. Their manufacture consumes one-third of our natural resources, uses up one-third of our energy supply and costs one-third of an average income.

A house today must have, at the least, a two-car garage. (For larger homes, three- and four-

154

car garages are common, and I have had requests from clients for ten- and twelve-car garages.) For the moderate-size house, this means the garage may be bigger than the living room. The largest area in the house is no longer the space in which the family lives but the space in which it stores its automobiles. When this huge storage box faces the entry side of the house it creates a street of unattractive garages rather than houses.

The impact of the garage on the proportions of a house is serious. Since many suburban lots today are quite narrow, a two-car garage that faces the street will become the most prominent architectural feature of a house. A side-opening garage is a much better choice than a front-opening one. This allows the street elevation of the house to actually look like a home for people, not just cars. It is also much safer if you don't have to back your car out into the street.

Most communities will not allow homeowners to leave their garage doors open because the view within is invariably unsightly. The usual view is a "hellhole" of boxes, bikes and belongings. A remote control device solves this problem.

Since cars are designed to be watertight, Wright believed they only needed to be covered, not crated. His solution was to provide a car shelter, for which he coined the word "carport." He extended the carport roof as a cantilever, thus adding to the sense of shelter that was characteristic of his houses.

The horizontal line of the carport roof also helps relate the house to the plane of the earth. Since no walls or doors are needed for a carport, this is a way to budget more construction dollars for the habitable part of the home.

American cars in general are no longer as bulky as the monsters of the fifties, and the influence of foreign car design has slenderized and improved American designs. But many families today have an SUV, a minivan, or a pickup truck. These require more space than passenger cars, necessitating higher and wider garage doors. People may want to store a boat and trailer in their garage, a camper or even a motor home. Some want a separate door for their golf cart.

The garage is also a place to store bicycles and trash bins, garden tools and a myriad of other items. We all collect "stuff." This used to be stored in the attic or basement; these areas may be omitted in contemporary designs, so the garage needs to be large enough to act as a mini-warehouse. Many garages include a space for a small workbench.

If the floor of the garage has a three-inch change in level placed just where the front wheels should stop, this makes it easier to park in the proper place. The floor of the garage should pitch slightly so that water will drain out under the garage door.

The front door is often used only by guests, because so many people coming home park their car in the garage and enter the home from there. Since they may be carrying groceries, the kitchen needs to be located nearby. Whenever possible, I try to plan a house so that one passes from the garage through a utility room (which doubles as a mudroom and laundry) into the entry hall. The kitchen should be in close proximity.

Although the automobile is a great liberating element and it is hard to imagine being without it, a family of moderate resources should reflect on its priorities. One wonders about our sense of value when we care more about our vehicle than the quality of our home.

You know you're in Southern California if the store is across the street and you drive there.
— Anonymous

STORAGE

I hate women because they always know where things are.

—James Thurber

We live in an affluent society. There are few people in the Western world who, in their lifetime, do not accumulate a sizeable amount of personal possessions. Although we may make a conscious effort to recycle, pass on or discard the many things that come into our possession, over the years we find ourselves gathering more and more "stuff." If you are one of the few who can truly say, "A place for everything and everything in its place," and then walk right to what you want in your house, you are among the chosen.

Every now and then someone down the street has a garage sale, usually when they are moving to another location. This becomes a temptation to buy things we may not need but can't afford to pass up. They are such bargains. Many are trapped just by the word "sale."

Where and how to store it all? The garage is the first place that comes to mind, as well as the basement and attic. But many houses that are built today have no attic or basement. A prefabricated metal shed that can be put up in the back or side yard is a storage solution — but unsightly. Off-site storage is another possibility. The problem with this is that we usually forget what we have stored there. Boxes pile up and anything that we want to

Opposite: *A ladder may be required to reach some shelves.*

Left: *A corridor is a good place for storage cabinets.*

retrieve is inevitably at the back or on the bottom. There is also the problem of leaks, fire, moths, mildew and rodents.

We all know we should resolve to accumulate less and eliminate more. If you are planning a new home, this is a good time for a critical review. An architect can help solve the problem by designing efficient ways to organize your storage. There are essential things we use daily — food, pots and pans, china, clothing, books, files, collections, toys and so forth. Then there are things we may use only once or twice a year and stuff that we think we may pass on to our children in the years ahead.

If you are going to build a new home, this is the time to take a few hours to do some planning and organize your storage needs. If you have a major problem, remember that there are consultants who specialize in storage solutions and books devoted to the subject.

To minimize the frustration of living amid clutter and spending inordinate amounts of time trying to find things, I suggest that you categorize what you need to store. Relate your storage needs to activities — cooking, dining, recreation, collections and hobbies. Some items are seasonal — clothes and equipment such as bikes and skis. Consider the size and shape of stored items, lighting requirements and whether items need to be readily available, concealed or displayed.

To be effective, a storage area should be

Top: *Storage cabinets can be both accessible and attractive.*

Above: *Windows above cabinets bring in daylight.*

designed to fit the particular space requirements of the item being stored. It should take into consideration ease of access, frequency of use, proximity to where it will be used, flexibility and security. Thoughtful design of storage space will save energy and reduce frustration. Remember that access to storage areas for children should be in scale with their height.

Some storage (such as magazines) is temporary. The aspect of recycling is another consideration, since items such as scrap paper and metal should be stored temporarily in bins. We used to store all sorts of letters and documents but many of these are now becoming electronic files that take up no physical space.

Items that you need to use frequently should be stored at, or near, waist height. Some storage shelves should be adjustable. Bookshelves are an opportunity to integrate furnishings and architecture.

Sometimes I design houses with few walk-in closets. Instead there are lots of reach-in closets. These storage units can extend continuously down the window side of the bedroom-wing corridor. They can be just over five feet tall by two feet deep. The space above can be a series of windows, which provide daylight to the corridor. Bedrooms can also have reach-in closets. Since all stored items are in sight and reachable, the method is quite efficient.

At the bottom of these closets I include a recessed toespace, which lifts the closet doors off the floor and also provides an opportunity for lighting (such as Ropelight). To guard against moths, it is a good idea to line closets with red cedar, which is available as plywood or boards.

Another space-saving storage place is below built-in seats. Under the seat cushion is a hinged or lift-out plywood panel, with empty space below. Even hassocks can be designed to have lift-out seats and storage space.

Try to locate storage areas where they are most useful — close to the place where you need the stored items. Some places you may not have thought about. Pull-out drawers below your bed for extra blankets or a cabinet above the water closet for storing toilet paper.

Put a full-length mirror on the back of a closet door. Or, if you have three tall closet doors next to each other, put mirrors on them and hinge them so as to create a three-way mirror.

Every cubic inch of space is a miracle.

—Walt Whitman

Left: *Reach-in closets are an alternative to walk-in closets.*

Right: *Cabinets with a flush front are less fussy.*

SUSTAINABLE DESIGN

In every deliberation, we must consider the impact of our decisions on the next seven generations.
—The Great Law of the Iroquois Confederacy

Sustainable design in housing means building sensibly now while carefully considering the legacy we are leaving to our children and their children. If we really had vision we would be spending more effort on long-range planning. What wisdom to be thinking ahead for seven generations. Few people today plan more than a year ahead and some can't get beyond the weekend.

Robert C. Gilman said, "Think of sustainability as extending the Golden Rule over time, so you do to future generations as you would have them do to you." When we build our house we should remember it is part of a much bigger picture. There is an interaction between our home, our community, the economy and the environment.

Many thoughtful people appreciate Dr. James Lovelock's idea of a global entity, which he calls Gaia (from the ancient Greek Earth-Goddess). Looking at the evolution of earth and life over billions of years, the theory of Gaia sees our planet as a unified, self-regulating, living superorganism that maintains a dynamic balance of nature. The conditions necessary for an environment that is hospitable to all forms of life are kept in balance through a cooperative process, rather than a competitive one.

Natural instincts in some species of animals and insects lead them to build. Birds construct nests, rodents dig tunnels, beavers create dams, spiders spin webs. They are genuine architects and builders responding to their environment. They have refined their methods over countless years by trial and error, and they can teach us something about architecture.

Primitive humans were protected by thick skin and a coat of hair. Over the centuries, as our

Opposite: *Timeless architecture is an essential aspect of sustainable design.*

*Use trees to shade
exterior walls.*

*Use roof overhangs to
shade walls and windows.*

skin grew tender, we needed to find some form of defense against the elements. One of our first accomplishments on this earth was the ability to construct a shelter. The first form of shelter was a cave, which provided some protection from the weather and predatory beasts. But weather was not the only thing that we needed to protect ourselves against. We were forever at war with each other, and our shelters often took the form of castles and fortresses. Sometimes entire towns were protected by walls or moats. In China a wall was built to protect an entire country.

Since most of them didn't work, we eventually gave up these defensive structures (in which only a privileged few could live) and started to build structures whose main protection was against the elements of Nature. But now that we feel relatively free from the threat of war, have we learned to live in harmony with our environment? And have we thought about the impact we are having on the future of our planet?

As we depend so heavily on industry, science and technology to support our lifestyle, we must consider the impact on our planet earth and the legacy that we leave to future generations. Not many of us are thinking about the global effect that our actions will have on our grandchildren, and their grandchildren. As we turn on the lights, adjust the thermostat, read the newspaper, watch TV, drive our car and fly across the country, do many of us remember we are using up our finite natural resources at an ever increasing rate? It took billions of years for nature to create oil and coal. It will take us only 150 more years to deplete them. It takes several lifetimes to grow mature hardwood trees. For years we clear-cut our forests without replanting them. In some cases we changed the balance of ecology so radically that all the topsoil was eroded and no new forest was possible.

162

Every hour of the day, the human race increases by 8,700 people. In the next thirty years, the world population of six billion is expected to double. The world our children and grand-children inherit is going to be profoundly affected by our actions today.

Fortunately, more people are taking on the responsibility of developing sustainable solutions. It all starts with education, and education starts with parents. If parents and schools will take the time to enlighten our children about the essential need to live in harmony with our environment, future generations will learn ways to live on this earth without destroying it.

According to L. Hunter Lovins and Amory B. Lovins of the Rocky Mountain Institute, in their books *Natural Capitalism* and *Energy Unbound,* there are four principles that must be applied if we are to heal our planet:

1. We need to increase resource productivity. In the U.S. we have an annual energy expense of $500 billion but $300 billion of it is wasted. Already, several major companies have demonstrated that by increasing energy efficiency they can increase profits.

2. We need to eliminate the concept of waste. The Lovins pose the question — how clean would a city make the water it discharges if its intake pipes were downstream of its outlets? Like it or not, we all live downstream.

3. We need to shift the structure of the economy from focusing on production and sales to a continuous flow of service and value. This provides an incentive to eliminate waste because provider and customer make money by finding more efficient solutions that benefit both. Home products and services, ranging from carpets to air conditioning, could be leased, maintained and eventually recycled, at a lower cost than under conventional methods.

Minimize waste

4. We need to invest in the reversal of the worldwide destruction of the ecosystem. True capitalists should restore nature where it is degraded and sustain it where it is healthy — the better to create wealth and sustain life.

WEATHER

Mark Twain's adage, "Everybody complains about the weather but nobody does anything about it," is still true. We can, however, control the "weather" within our house, meaning our environmental conditions. The type of weather in the area in which you live should have an impact on the design of your home, and especially on the sort of roof that you put on your house.

Although we often may wish we lived in a perpetually balmy climate, we would probably get bored with the world if the weather were perfect every day of the year. Seasonal changes in the weather make life more interesting. If winter is too cold or summer too hot, a little suffering adds some spice to life. In the movie, *Teahouse of the August Moon,* Marlon Brando, playing a native Okinawan, said, "Suffering makes man think, thought makes man wise, and wisdom makes life endurable."

Those of us who live in the Sunbelt of the United States don't have to shovel snow, but the

Utilize natural daylighting.

Design for space efficiency.

change of seasons is not very dramatic. We don't see much of the miracle of spring or appreciate the joy of a clear sky after weeks of rain.

SOLAR ENERGY

The miracle of energy delivered by the sun is largely overlooked. Each day it pours down vast quantities of light and heat, yet few homeowners take much advantage of it. If we were told that gasoline was being given away, the street would be full of cars lined up to take advantage of such an amazing event. Yet the amount of free solar energy that falls on the roof of an average house is more than three times the amount of power required to run an energy-efficient home. It could power our lights, air conditioning and kitchen appliances.

We have become so used to having energy delivered to our home by the utility company that we have devoted little effort to harnessing energy from the sun — solar energy.

Solar energy can be used passively or actively. Using it passively means designing your house with good common sense. No special equipment is involved and it is the ultimate in low technology.

Your house should be oriented to acknowledge the path of the sun and its different paths in summer and winter. Plan the location of rooms in your house accordingly. Extend roofs out to shade walls. Utilize clerestory windows and skylights. Consider earth berms and planted shade trees. An effective solution is the solar hemicycle house, which is shaped in an arc so as to track the path of the sun through the sky.

The best thing about passive solar design is it that doesn't cost any more to begin with and it works every day to keep you comfortable. It doesn't pollute and it requires no maintenance. There are three principles behind passive solar design:

Design for longevity.

1. A house should be built with thermal integrity to maintain a level of human comfort through a range of external conditions.
2. It should accept solar heat and light in certain ways and places but reject them in others.
3. It should have the ability to retain either the presence or absence of heat or cooling.

We have not yet found the most cost-effective ways to harvest the power of the sun, but are closing the gap. Today, providing "active" solar energy for a moderate-size house calls for an investment of about $20,000 and payback takes from twelve to eighteen years. Too much and too long, but it will get better. As the demand for world energy continues to increase and the supply of fossil fuels is further depleted, we will have to depend more and more on this abundant energy source. Photovoltaics, a process that converts solar energy directly into electricity, should become a significant way to energize our houses.

ALTERNATIVE ENERGY

There are many ways to produce energy other than through the use of fossil fuels. Wind and water have been sources of energy since ancient times.

Windmills are low technology and in many rural areas of the U.S. are used to pump water

Use durable materials. and generate electricity. If you happen to live next to a river, a water wheel is worth considering. Other natural sources of energy are the ocean tides and geothermal wells. For the average homeowner these are interesting but probably not applicable.

Let's hope that we will soon see the development of fuel cells, which use only hydrogen and oxygen to produce electrical energy. In the future they will probably energize our cars and eventually our homes at a low cost without creating any pollution.

ATOMIC ENERGY

With improved safety assurances, nuclear energy is a player once again. Operating procedures have been refined to raise its "capacity factor" (actual output compared to potential output) to ninety percent. Compare this with coal plants, which run at a factor of sixty-one percent and oil and natural gas generators, which run at ten to twenty-nine percent. Atomic energy is already producing twenty percent of the nation's electricity. At less than half a cent per kilowatt hour, electricity from nuclear plants is far less expensive than coal, oil or natural gas, which run between two and four cents per kWh. The "pebble bed modular reactor" promises increased safety, lower plant construction costs and less radioactive waste.

Fossil fuels will start to run out in a few generations, but the demand for electricity in the U.S. is expected to rise thirty percent in the next twenty years.

GLOBAL WARMING

If you listen to media hype and zealous environmentalists, our world is rapidly committing suicide by not placing immediate and severe limits on the emissions of carbon dioxide and other greenhouse gases. Truth is, the alarm that they spread is not based on scientific studies or facts. Over 17,000 meteorologists, climatologists, physicists and environmental scientists have signed a petition opposing the supposition that human release of greenhouse gases such as carbon dioxide and methane is warming the earth's atmosphere. A United Nations study on global warming, argued MIT climate scientist Richard Lindzen, came from taking "scenarios with horrific and unimaginable emissions and putting them in the most sensitive computer simulation model." Sallie Baliunas of Harvard University's Smithsonian Center for Astrophysics states, "Prophecies of calamitous human-caused warming are exaggerated. Our planet is about one degree Fahrenheit warmer today than it was a century ago but it was much warmer a thousand years ago, long before the Industrial Revolution."

Part of the drive to reduce energy use in the home and elsewhere derives from concern about global warming. The issue needs to be more carefully and objectively analyzed so that we can determine reasonable and economically sound methods to curb greenhouse gases.

AIR

We take many things for granted, including the air that we breathe. Those who live in or near urban areas can no longer do so. Industries around the world have been slow at recognizing their impact on the environment. We now manufacture over 80,000 chemicals in the world, yet less than half of them have been tested for toxicity to humans. We know little about the long-term effects of most of these chemicals on our health, except that there has been a dramatic rise in cancer, infertility and learning disabilities in children in the past century.

Many of the products with which we build our homes are made with chemicals. Do we think all these chemicals stay permanently sealed in and never leak into the air? If you have just installed a new carpet or had your house painted, you will remember how strong the smells were at first. After a while we just get used to them.

We frequently shut our windows tight because the outside air is filled with smog. We are

Use high-performance windows.

A smaller house uses fewer materials and consumes less energy.

also advised to build a house that is virtually airtight, so as to reduce the amount of energy it takes to heat or cool it. However, in so doing we subject ourselves to chemical emissions from inside our house — from paint, glues, plastics, fabrics and other synthetic materials. We should be able to bring some fresh air into our home periodically.

WATER

Besides the air we breathe, water is another essential that we tend to take for granted. A person can survive for several weeks without food but only a few days without water. In the Western world, we are notoriously wasteful of water, our most valuable asset. A joint study financed by the U.S. and Japan found that the greatest single global threat to food production and human health over the next twenty-five years will be a shortage of water; 1.3 billion people in the world currently have no access to clean water.

In the sunshine states, we use enormous amounts of water for golf courses, much of which could be saved if we recycled wastewater from our homes. We use 4,776 gallons of water to grow a Christmas tree, 39,000 gallons to manufacture an automobile.

Residential water use in much of the country is higher than commercial or industrial use. The biggest guzzler is the toilet, followed by showers and washing machines. We think nothing of taking a long shower or leaving a garden hose running all night. We can't imagine not having enough water.

Although there are water closets on the market that flush efficiently with reduced amounts of water, not all of them are recommended because some have to be flushed several times, thus negating their alleged water-use efficiency.

THINGS WE CAN DO

If we do not take more responsibility now and set a better example of caring for our planet, we will have passed on a terrible legacy to future generations, one that could be irreversible. It is a human trait to take an interest in only the tangible things that affect our everyday life.

To take an interest in our neighbors, our community, our country and our planet means escaping from this narrow thinking.

Ecology is the term we use to describe the study of the pattern of relations between organisms and their environment. "Green architecture" means architecture that is environmentally responsible, and a sustainable house means one with a high-performance design.

Some simple things can make the design of a home sustainable:

- Orient the house to take the best advantage of sun and wind.
- Save existing trees and natural vegetation.
- Plant more trees and shrubs, especially on the east and west sides of your house.
- Manage drainage on your site so as to prevent soil erosion.
- Design for space efficiency. A smaller house uses less material, takes less effort to maintain and consumes less energy.
- Design for longevity. Avoid styles that come and go.
- Keep designs simple with fewer corners.
- Minimize waste. Design with an appreciation for the standard sizes of building materials.
- Use engineered wood instead of solid lumber.
- Use durable and low-maintenance materials that don't require painting.
- Use weather-stripping.
- Use roof overhangs and trees to shade exterior walls.
- Provide natural cross ventilation.
- Use natural daylighting.
- Design for passive solar heating.
- Use solar hot water heating and photovoltaics (as they become cost effective).
- Install high-efficiency heating and cooling equipment.
- Use thermostatic controls that automatically adjust to seasons and day/night cycles.
- Provide a high level of thermal insulation.
- Use high-performance windows and glass with a low solar heat gain.
- Use water-efficient plumbing fixtures — toilets, showerheads and faucets.
- Provide storage bins for recyclable materials — aluminum cans, paper and glass.
- Seek alternatives to chemical pesticides and ozone-depleting materials.

Gradually we are becoming aware of our responsibility to protect Planet Earth and conserve its natural resources. Those who work at home will save on fossil fuels consumed in travel. Sustainable design, as it applies to your home, is largely a matter of common sense. It has to do with the design of your house, its construction and the energy it will require for operation and maintenance.

Man shapes himself through decisions that shape his environment.

—René Dubos

Consider the legacy we are leaving to our children.

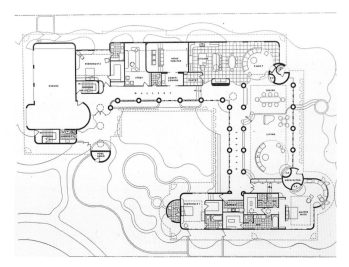

ENVIRONMENTAL SYSTEMS

Air conditioning is the reconciliation of extremes.

—FLLW

Environmental systems are the methods we use to temper the climate inside our homes and maintain it at comfortable levels. They include heating, ventilating, air conditioning, plumbing and electrical. Most homes built today have all-year air conditioning which includes both heating and cooling. In the past fifty years, science and technology have come a long way toward making our house more comfortable.

Human comfort is largely an individual matter. Some people are tolerant of higher or lower temperatures, while others are more sensitive. What is a cooling breeze to some is an unpleasant draft to others. The sense of comfort involves many factors other than air temperature. If we remember our high school physics, heat travels by convection (air movement), by conduction (up the handle of a frying pan, for instance), and by radiation (from the sun, for example). The human body loses about eighty percent of its heat from convection and radiation, twenty percent through evaporation and virtually none through conduction.

Comfort is not just a matter of ambient air temperature. There is the factor of mean radiant temperature. This is what we experience when it is freezing outside but we feel warm when we stand in the sun. It is the radiant heat from the sun that warms us. Cold air is not the determining comfort factor but the rate at which our bodies absorb heat.

The human body is itself an amazing environmental system, opening and closing pores and adjusting the amount of perspiration according to fluctuations in temperature and humidity. Perspiration is the way our bodies cool through the process of evaporation. When water (sweat) evaporates into the air it loses heat so our bodies feel cooler. A cotton shirt feels more

We use science and technology to make our homes more comfortable.

A house should be oriented with consideration of the forces of nature.

Below: *Take advantage of prevailing breezes.*

comfortable in hot weather than one made of a synthetic material because it allows perspiration to escape into the atmosphere.

It is usually assumed by designers of heating and cooling systems that the comfort zone is in the seventy to eighty degree Fahrenheit range as long as the relative humidity lies between twenty and fifty percent. If there is adequate air circulation, eighty-five degrees or higher will still be comfortable. At seventy-five and eighteen percent relative humidity we are comfortable, but at this moderate temperature we are uncomfortable if the humidity goes up to sixty percent and there is no air movement.

What common-sense things can be done in the design of your home to increase your comfort level? To start with, the orientation of your house should take into consideration all the forces of nature — the sun, the wind and the types of precipitation. In moderate amounts these are all beneficial. Your fuel bills will be much lower if your house is sited to take the best advantage of solar heat and light and if it has roof overhangs to shade the walls and windows. If there are prevailing breezes on your property you may want to slow them down or speed them up. This can be done by using trees, hedges and shrubs as either windbreaks (perpendicular to the prevailing wind) or as wind funnels (parallel to the wind). You may wish to incorporate a breezeway in the design of your house so as to capture natural air movement. A breezeway can be designed so as create a Venturi effect, which accelerates the air velocity.

There are many choices of air conditioning equipment available today. Since all systems need to be adjusted from time to time and repaired or replaced, be sure the system you select is made by a reputable manufacturer and that prompt and adequate service is available. Your air conditioning system should keep the temperature and humidity at a comfortable level, adjusting to the time of day and season of the year. Micro-filters will remove dust and pollen, electrostatic filters will ionize and clean the air.

The most common system for residences is the forced air heating and cooling system. A furnace heats air with a flame from gas or oil, or by using electric resistance coils. The furnace may be upflow, with ducts above the ceiling, or downflow, with ducts below the floor. They will need an intake for combustion air. If space is tight, a horizontal-type furnace takes up less room. Cooling can be provided by adding evaporator coils in the ductwork and an outdoor compressor and condensing unit. Some quantity of fresh air should be introduced into the system.

A heat pump employs a reversible refrigeration cycle to either heat or cool. It is an economical solution but if the temperature outside falls below freezing you may need to include electrical resistance coils (which will increase your fuel bill). Heat pumps may also use water or earth as a heat source.

As discussed previously, solar heating can be accomplished

Above: *Thermally superior glass dramatically reduces heating and cooling costs.*

Left: *Solar angles for your site change with the season and time of day.*

Divide your home into zones with individual controls for each zone.

through either a passive or an active system. The former is incorporated in the design and orientation of the house. An active system requires special equipment, including a backup system for sunless periods, that may be hard to accommodate aesthetically. A passive system is worth considering, especially in northern climates, as it may reduce fuel costs, but at present, active systems are rarely cost-effective.

An effective distribution method that provides a combination of gravity heat and forced warm air is provided by the Airfloor system. Instead of pipes in the slab that circulate hot water, the system consists of two-way ducts created by metal forms that are placed before the concrete slab is poured. This method provides both gravity heat and air circulation.

Hydronic systems circulate hot water instead of air, and distribute heat into rooms with radiators or fin-tube convectors (which can have fans to help distribute the air).

One of the most important things you can do when building a moderate-cost home is to find a better solution than mounting a package air conditioning unit on the roof where it is exposed to view. Better to use a split system mounted on the ground, where the condensing unit can be hidden by a fence or wall. If you must use a roof-mounted unit, at least put a screen around it.

An economical way to cool is the evaporative method, but it works only in hot, dry climates. Evaporative coolers, while economical to install and operate, require regular yearly maintenance. When the humidity rises, they don't cool effectively.

Control systems can be quite sophisticated. Thermostats turn equipment on and off at designated preset temperatures (just remember that turning a thermostat up to a higher number doesn't make it provide heat faster). Thermostats can be linked to time clocks to turn heating or cooling on at predetermined times. Some control systems can be programmed for days ahead and even to respond to a telephone call. Using the telephone or Internet, we can speak to our home from a remote distance, checking on its condition and changing or reprogramming its control systems. But check out the costs first. It may take decades to repay the investment.

Dividing your house into zones is a good idea because then you can adjust the amount of air and control the temperature in different parts of your home individually, especially the living and sleeping areas. In some colder climates where heating is required, you may find a humidifier is appropriate.

After you leave your home unattended for a few weeks you probably wonder where all the dust comes from. Indoor air pollution, according to the Environmental Protection Agency, is one of the top five urgent environmental risks to public health.

I suggest you use the highest quality filters available. Some types are washable, others are the throwaway kind. Dust, smog, smoke and other airborne particles can be effectively reduced by using high-capacity micropore filters. A good filter has electrostatic fibers to trap most of the airborne dust, smoke and allergens. A charcoal filter will help purify the air.

Replaceable filters need to be changed every few months, depending on how clogged up they become. There are also small, freestanding fan units with throwaway filters that circulate and clean the air within a room.

There are a few simple things to remember about plumbing. Be sure you know where the main shutoff valves are located for water and gas. If you have a two-story house, you will save money if bathrooms on the second floor align with those below. Avoid having a bed placed against a wall that has a water closet from somebody else's bathroom. Be sure to record where the cleanouts in the drains are located. If you have a bathroom in the basement and it is below the level of the sewer line, you will have to install a sewage ejector pump. If you have a septic system it will eventually need to be pumped out. Be careful about planting trees near sewer lines because roots seek water and can cause havoc with drain lines. Be sure that plumbing vents are not located close to windows or air intakes.

As for the electrical system, an underground electric utility line is far preferable to wires stretched from a pole to your roof. Walk through your house when the framing is almost complete and while the wiring is being installed. Check that wall switches, convenience outlets and lighting fixtures are being installed where you want them. Do this before the finish surface is installed because it will be costly to move them or add more later. The mechanics who install your heating, air conditioning, plumbing and electrical systems are all governed by building codes and their work is (or should be) inspected before it is covered up with finish materials.

A house is a machine in which to live but architecture begins where that concept of the house ends. All life is machinery in a rudimentary sense, and yet machinery is the life of nothing.

—FLLW

Use the highest quality air filters that are available.

INTERIORS

The reality of a building consists not of the four walls but the space within to be lived in.

—Laotse

I don't believe we should make any distinction between exterior and interior design. This approach, I am convinced, goes a long way towards creating a better design. The interior of a house should be completely compatible with its exterior. Only when the inside and outside are in complete harmony do we have something we can call architecture. Let me try to describe a way to integrate the process.

My design concept for a home invariably starts with the idea of interior space. Instead of first defining exterior walls and then dividing the inside space up into rooms, I visualize the various spaces that will be appropriate to serve the different activities of the family, thinking of interesting ways to relate them to each other. In this process, form and function become one and the same. When a home is designed from the inside out, the exterior form of the house becomes a natural consequence of interior space.

I mentally take on the role of each member of the family and place myself in their shoes. In my imagination I became the homeowner, greeting guests, cooking and serving meals, tending the children, having a conversation or reading a book.

The design process should always proceed from generals to particulars. Major issues must be identified first. The details follow and became an integral part of the whole.

The central feature of a home is apt to be the fireplace in the living room. This is an opportunity for a sculptural design. It is usually constructed from masonry — stone, brick or concrete block. It becomes an "anchor" for the home, both structurally and philosophically. The main seating area in the living room is then focused on the fireplace, and if there is a significant exterior

The interior of a home should be in harmony with the exterior.

A home office should be both functional and beautiful.

view available, this is taken into account. The interior space is usually arranged so that the fire can also be enjoyed from the dining area.

I believe that good design does not follow a linear-thinking approach, considering just one factor at a time, but uses a method that we might call parallel processing. Starting from the interior space where the family lives, I incorporate in the design concept all the aspects of the site — the landforms, the vegetation, the views and the weather patterns. Some of the inside surfaces, walls, floors and ceilings will extend through to the outside to expand the interior space. This is the way to achieve a sense of integrity in a design. Nothing is tacked on as an afterthought.

Some designers create a room by defining where the walls are located and then letting somebody else figure out how to fit everything in — choose the furniture, pick the color schemes, and select the floor and wall coverings. My preliminary floor plans indicate where the furniture is best placed. When the construction drawings are prepared, I include details for most of the furnishings in the house, specifying the type, texture and color for the finish materials — floors, walls and ceilings. A landscaping plan is also included.

Every piece of furniture was custom designed.

For the living room, I like to provide a design for a built-in seat. Since this takes up less room than a sofa, it is a space saver. The seat can be made by the carpenters who build the house, making it less expensive than furniture from a store. The plans will include details for built-in cabinets throughout the house.

Drawings sometimes include designs for freestanding items of furniture, such as the living room chairs, coffee and side tables, dining table and chairs, beds, nightstands and built-in lighting fixtures. In some cases I have designed upholstery and carpets.

Your home should be easy to maintain and the interior arrangements flexible enough so that some changes can be made as time goes by.

We had constant lessons in interior design from Mr. Wright, who had an almost compulsive need to rearrange furniture. When he traveled between Taliesin and Taliesin West, one of the first things he would do would be to relocate the furniture. Chairs, tables, beds would all find new positions. Apprentices would get a good workout, especially when we had to move grand pianos. Nothing was sacred. The desks in the studio would be moved into different positions every year.

One day he was arranging the dining room furniture by himself. I walked in and thought I might be of use. There was a tall oriental pot standing in the corner. Mr. Wright reached over, picked it up in one hand and held it out to me. "Let's put this over there," he said. I took it in both arms and immediately staggered under its weight. I had forgotten how physically strong he was.

A teak coffee table with a marble inlay.

Below: *The color scheme is designed to add warmth to the room.*

One of his clients, Jorgine Boomer, had an apartment in New York at the Waldorf Astoria. She suggested the Wrights use it next time they were in the city. After the first night there, they decided to do her a favor and rearrange the furniture. They stayed up half the night moving everything — sofas, chairs, tables and lamps. When they departed they left a note for Jorgine. Their efforts, unfortunately, were not appreciated, and everything was quickly restored to its original position.

The card table has swing-out trays for drinks.

ACOUSTICS

A subject few people consider in the design of a home is acoustics. Good acoustics mean that you can hear voices and music clearly. You don't want a lot of reverberations and echoes that distort sound.

There are some simple solutions to controlling these. When sound strikes a hard surface, it is reflected. If it strikes a soft surface, it is absorbed. When it is reflected, it behaves just as light does — the angle of incidence equals the angle of reflection. If you are in a room with two hard-surfaced walls that are parallel, sounds (people speaking or music) may become garbled because echoes are criss-crossing your ear. So the shape of a room has a lot to do with acoustics. Circular or box-shaped rooms need special consideration.

If you plan to watch TV or listen to, or perhaps even perform, music in the living room you should be aware of the acoustical properties of the space. Avoid having too many hard surfaces that will reflect sound. Be careful of large expanses of hard-surfaced floors and ceilings in living, dining and sleeping areas. Use soft surfaces to soak up sound, such as wood, carpets and fabric — drapery and upholstery.

NOISE CONTROL

Noise is unwanted sound. Some comes from outside your house. If you live near a highway, you may need to deal with traffic noise. This is especially true if you are near a highway stop sign where large trucks use air brakes. If your neighbors are very close you may have a different sort of noise problem to control.

There are also internal noises that need to be controlled. One of these is the cocktail party, which can be one of the loudest of all events. In order to hear each other, everybody starts speaking louder, and a few drinks encourages this.

One reason I separated the children's and parents' rooms in the '97 Life Dream House was so that the children could play loud music without offense.

If your home is in the path of low-flying jets or near a busy highway you may have to think of ways to attenuate these noises. A masonry wall will stop noise more effectively than a stud wall.

If your bed shares the same wall as a water closet you will have a problem. A simple and effective wall that blocks sound is made by "staggering" the studs and putting a double layer of drywall on one face.

STAIRS AND RAMPS

An observant architect in the past commented that architecture would be easy if there were no need for stairs or roofs.

Bookshelves and storage cabinets also include stereo equipment.

If you want sensible steps, remember the formula: the vertical height of the riser multiplied by horizontal width of the tread should equal between seventy and seventy-five. For interior stairs, I make the risers six inches high and the tread twelve inches wide. This ratio is comfortable to climb or descend, for both adults and children. It also agrees with the formula: A six-inch riser times a twelve-inch tread equals seventy-two. Risers that are higher than eight inches are too steep.

Treads should have a non-skid surface and a nosing that projects out slightly from the face of the step. An alternative is to slope the riser out at an angle (this is also good for carpeted stairs).

Since stairs occupy a lot of space, sometimes a spiral stair may be useful as a secondary means of vertical travel.

Outdoors, I like to use "monumental" steps that are four inches high and sixteen inches wide. These are easy to walk up, especially for the physically challenged, older people, children and pets (even though they don't fit the formula). In some cases they are good indoors, such as in a sunken living room.

I never use a single step since it creates the danger of tripping. When a small change in level is required, I use at least three steps or a shallow ramp. Stairs with more than three steps should have handrails. Long stair runs should be broken up with a landing.

The family room is a place to sit back and put your feet up.

Carpets should be laid so as not to come loose. Stairs should be well lit. A skylight or window provides daylight, and built-in steplights and overhead or wall lights provide light at night.

Ramps are a convenient way to get from one level to another and often necessary for those who have difficulty walking. Their drawback is that they take up a lot of space. A ramp that slopes at a ratio of one to twelve will take up twelve feet in length just to rise one foot. Outdoors where there is more space they make good sense.

ACCESSIBILITY

This is an issue that should be considered in the design of a house. Even though there are no legal requirements to make your home ADA compliant, if you plan on living there for some time you should think about how you would get around in a wheelchair if you broke a leg.

Years ago I spent a several weeks in a wheelchair. It was an enlightening education. I think all architects should spend at least one day like this so they can appreciate the problem.

For people with more permanent locomotion problems, there are residential-size elevators and chair lifts that run up the side of stairs. Today, architects employ the process of "universal design," which takes a broader look and considers how changes in mobility, agility and perceptual acuity of family members from childhood to adulthood need to be incorporated in a home.

If you are building a two- or three-story home, consider locating closets on each floor that are stacked vertically. In the future, you could use the space to install a small elevator. There may be places where ramps are appropriate.

HARDWARE

There are two basic types of hardware — rough hardware such as nails, screws and joist hangers, and finish hardware, such as doorknobs, hinges and cabinet pulls and catches. Years ago I ran across a book titled, *Taking the Mystery Out of Hardware.* I patiently waded through it and ended up by being more mystified than ever. A visit to your local builder's hardware store will expose you to a bewildering array of possibilities.

My recommendation is to keep everything simple. Show as little hardware as possible. For the front door, consider using a hardwood knob instead of metal. It feels warmer to the touch, and offers a friendlier "handshake" to your guests. Some people put their front door knob in the center of the door but this makes it awkward to open.

A good type of hinge for your front door is the recessed offset pivot type (more common to commercial use). Since it is difficult to weatherstrip it is best if the door is set back under a deep roof overhang.

For cabinet hardware, I prefer continuous piano hinge. It helps prevent the doors from warping and it looks good. If warping is not a problem, use offset pivot hinges. They are inexpensive, easy to install and unobtrusive. They come in different sizes and work for small cabinets or large closet doors.

Have nothing in your house that you do not know to be useful, or believe to be beautiful.
—William Morris

The sunken area by the fireplace has a built-in seat.

LIGHT

To me every hour of the light and dark is a miracle.

—Walt Whitman

According to Genesis, the first thing God did when he brought the universe into existence was to create light. Most life on earth could not exist without it. Light is an intangible, and this makes it more difficult for designers to describe because we cannot show a client a sample board of "lighting effects."

There are two kinds of light to consider in the home — daylight (natural light) and artificial light. Both types can be delivered as direct, indirect or reflected, and they usually come in a mixture. All types of light need to be controlled.

DAYLIGHT

The sun is both our friend and our enemy. Not enough light and our physical and mental health suffer, crop growth is retarded and our houses are gloomy. Too much and our bodies cook, our skin burns and our eyes suffer from glare. Wood and fabrics dry out and fade. In the winter we are glad to have our houses warmed but in the summer it may be just the opposite.

On a clear day, sunlight lands on our house as direct light. When it strikes surfaces — the roof, walls or ground, some of it is reflected. If there is an overcast sky, light will be diffused. The most comfortable light is a blend of these types of light.

In designing a home, we have to take into account the sun's

Opposite: *The magic of light is most apparent at sunset.*

Below: *The lattice screen modifies the sun's rays but allows air movement.*

Above: *Daylight from clerestory windows is bounced up to the ceiling.*

Above right: *Clerestory windows give the roof a light, floating quality.*

Below: *Skylights are a way to bring daylight into the interior space.*

Below right: *Art glass panel in the skylight.*

position in the sky, which changes according to the time of day and season of the year. The sun brings us both light and heat, and does not send us a utility bill at the end of the month. But it must be controlled — we want neither too much nor too little. The most effective daylight controls start with the basic design of the house.

Skylights and Clerestories

A good way to illuminate interior spaces is with clerestory windows. Daylight introduced at this level will reflect off the ceiling and bring diffused light to the space below.

Skylights provide opportunities to bring natural daylight into areas of your home that would otherwise be dark and gloomy. The areas where they make the biggest contribution are by the fireplace in the living area, over the dining table, in the kitchen, your home office and over stairwells and dark entrances and hallways.

Skylights come in a variety of sizes and shapes — square, rectilinear, circular and triangular. Use ones that have thermal insulation (double or triple glazing). You should also specify UV (ultraviolet) shielding. For residences, the best types are acrylic or polycarbonate plastic, white transparent, self-flashing type. Operable skylights are available with manual or motor operation.

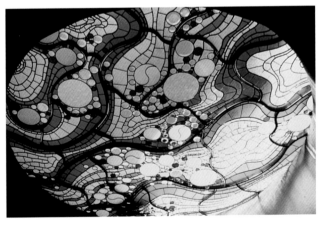

A skylight over the stairwell brings light down to the lower level.

In some houses I have designed stained glass panels that fit below the skylight (they have lights installed above so you can see the artglass at night).

ORIENTATION

Most city blocks are laid out on a north-south axis. Since many lots are not large enough for the house to be set at an angle, this results in houses having a dark side. A better orientation for your home is thirty to sixty degrees, so all sides get some sunlight.

Sidelights and art glass inserts bring daylight into the entry.

The location of rooms in relationship to the sun is also important. Morning sun in the bedrooms is preferable, and the living area should generally be on the south side. There are sometimes conditions that will change this, such as street access, lot size and shape, views, wind direction and so forth. You may also have your own preferences about light.

It has been proven that a lack of light can cause depression. Too much inside a house will fade the colors in fabrics. When sunlight is not controlled it can cause glare. Glare, which is uncomfortable brightness, can be caused by direct sunlight. It may also come from indirect light that bounces off a reflective surface such as a pool of water or a concrete terrace. This is something to remember if you are locating a pool or concrete slab near the house.

There are several ways to control natural light. You can use drapes or blinds, but this means spending time opening and closing them. You can use reflective glass, which may help you but cause a problem for your neighbor or people driving down the street. You can use tinted glass, which is like wearing sunglasses.

The simplest way to control light is to let the roof extend out beyond the walls. Since the sun is at a lower angle in the winter, the depth of the roof overhang can be designed to allow some winter sun to warm the home. In the summer, when the sun is higher in the sky, the eaves will provide shade.

ARTIFICIAL LIGHT

At night we depend on artificial light, which comes to us today chiefly thanks to Thomas Edison, who invented the incandescent light bulb just over a hundred years ago. Before that time our forebears had to use candles, kerosene lamps and firelight. Today we have a wide choice of lamps to select from when we light our homes. They vary in their light quality, color, intensity, energy consumed, cost and lifespan. We have not yet duplicated the quality of daylight, but are coming closer.

My own experience as the lighting designer in our Taliesin Theater gave me a special appreciation for the importance of good lighting. Although we know that our sight is precious, we often neglect it and subject our eyes to glare and strain. One of the simplest things we can do in our home is to provide for a balance between light and shade.

There are two basic ways to light our home:

1. Direct lighting, such as downlights (usually recessed ceiling fixtures) and task lights (such as desk lamps). A good place for downlighting is over the dining table. Recessed pinhole lights can be adjusted to light only the surface of the table and not shine directly on people. This direct lighting should then be supplemented with other lighting in the room (lighting that flatters the people).

Direct lighting is a good way to light paintings and other forms of art. Wallwashers provide direct lighting on a wall, and this in turn is reflected into a room as indirect light. A gold reflector in the lighting fixture will provide a warmer light.

A light shelf designed to light trophies and personal items.

2. Indirect lighting, such as uplights from a light cove or "deck." The deck is a device that keeps a room in scale, helps create a feeling of repose and provides a shelf for uplights. It is basically an extension of a lower ceiling beyond the face of a wall that continues on up to a higher ceiling. Decks and light coves are ideal ways to provide indirect lighting with either fluorescent strip lights (type WWX tubes are recommended over CW) or with strip lights such as Ropelight.

Another way to create indirect light is through wallwashers. These can be ceiling-mounted lights than shine on the wall, not the floor, or urn-type lights that are mounted on the wall.

Floor and table lamps can provide both direct and indirect lighting. Torchiere floor lamps are a flexible way to provide uplighting and usually come with a built-in dimmer switch.

Types of Artificial Lighting

Incandescent light bulbs create the warmest light. Fluorescent tubes use less energy, last longer than incandescent bulbs, but emit a cooler type of light. Fluorescent tubes come in different colors, ranging from CW (cool white) to WWX (warm white deluxe). The warmer colors are better in a house. In my home I use a mixture of incandescent and fluorescent lighting. The fluorescent lights are in a light cove and bounce light off the ceiling (indirect lighting). The downlights are recessed in the ceiling and provide direct lighting. To avoid changing bulbs frequently, I use the long-life type (20,000 hours).

I also have several floor lamps (torchieres) that bounce light off the ceiling. These use quartz halogen bulbs. They emit a whiter light but are very hot and must be kept away from curtains. The lamps have a tiny built-in dimmer. At night I turn them down so they just glow and they act as night-lights. Metal halide lights are appropriate for landscape lighting but should never be used indoors.

The choice of lighting types depends on the type of activity that is being lit and the ambience you want create in a particular space. To save your eyesight you should avoid watching TV in a dark room.

In your bathroom you want light that flatters skin tones, so use the incandescent type. Be sure to have a light in the ceiling that shines on the back of your head when you stand in front of the mirror (this is the way actors are lit on the stage). Don't start your day off by thinking how poorly you look when it's just the lighting that is bad.

In your kitchen you must have an adequate amount of light but remember that fluorescent light tends to make most food, especially meat, look unappetizing. A mixture of incandescent and WWX fluorescent will work.

The living area is best lit with indirect lighting combined with some downlights and floor and table lamps, with recessed pinhole ceiling lights over the dining table. In the Myers house we installed tiny fiber optic cables in the plaster ceiling of the dining room. In the daytime they cannot be seen. At night they make the ceiling glow like a starlit sky.

Bedroom lighting should have different settings, and if you read in bed you may want his-and-her lights and separate controls. Closets can have door-activated switches to turn on a light inside when the door is opened.

LIGHTING CONTROLS

These range from simple off-on wall switches to highly sophisticated electronic systems. Some types offer master controls of all the lights in your home from one or more locations. Some can be preprogrammed to turn selected lights on or off, at specified levels of brightness. Each room can be preset for different lighting modes, ranging from intimate to bright. Four preset modes are usually the right number — bright, softer, entertaining and TV. The Lutron Grafik Eye System is simple and moderate in cost.

There are sensors that automatically control the level of artificial light in our home, balancing it with varying amounts of daylight coming from windows and skylights. If you install a highly complicated system you may find it difficult to remember how to work it, but your children will probably come to your rescue.

Small dimmers that mount in a wall box are inexpensive. A simple way to reduce your monthly utility bill and extend the life of the lamp bulbs is to set the upper limit of the wall dimmer down a notch. Fluorescent lights can also be dimmed but this requires a special type of ballast in the fixture.

We reach for the light spiritually, as the plant does physically, if we are sound of heart and not sophisticated by our education.

—FLLW

A metal gate with translucent plexiglass and stained glass inserts.

LANDSCAPING

The good building makes the landscape more beautiful than it was before the building was built.

— FLLW

Landscape architecture is a subject that is taught separately in colleges and practiced as a discrete profession. However, I believe that all architects should have an understanding of landscape design.

Rather than just thinking about landscaping as what we do with the property around the house, let's start out by thinking of our home as part of a much larger landscaping scheme, one that extends far beyond the lot lines. If we live in the country, this is an easy thing to do. If we live in the suburbs, our "extended" landscape is going to include other houses, the street, vehicles, sidewalks and other evidence of "civilization." If we live in the city, we will be lucky if our environment includes anything at all that is natural.

Nevertheless, it is important to take the environment into account, since it has such a significant impact on our life and the design of our home.

Would you doubt the beneficial effect on our mental, physical and emotional health, and our ability to be productive, if our home environment included more trees and flowers (softscape) and less concrete and steel (hardscape)? Wouldn't we thrive if we had more fresh air and less smog?

We all have ideas about how to improve education. One of my suggestions is to get your young children into the garden with some seeds and a watering can. Let them participate in the miracle of watching a plant emerge from the soil, unfold in the sunlight, blossom and then go to seed. Let everyone plant a sapling in their youth so they can be proud of a mature tree in their senior years.

Opposite: *Trees provide shade and soften the hard lines of architecture.*

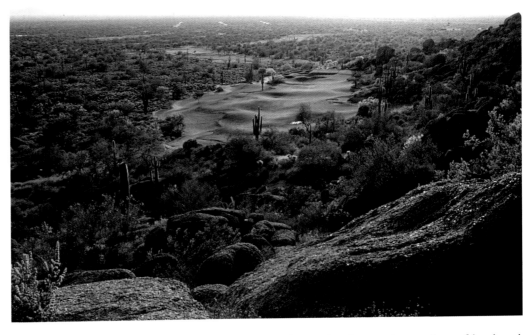

One of the tragedies of modern times occurs when a developer takes a piece of land and clears away all the vegetation in order to make it easier to construct roads and install utilities. Although this was standard procedure for many years, most communities today restrict this sort of devastation of the land, and a lot of effort is now put into preserving natural features. On a global scale, when we destroy the great rain forests we are threatening the future of life on our planet. Acting irresponsibly towards nature may cause an irreversible condition. Cutting down the great sandalwood forest in Hawaii caused all the topsoil to be washed away and reduced the amount of rainfall. Now there are virtually no sandalwood trees left on the islands.

*Soil erosion on a slope can
be controlled with plants.*

Many families today consist of parents who are both working, with little time available for watering or caring for a garden. There are many landscape services that will do this for you, and many plant species require minimal care. A garden that is carefully planned to provide color throughout the different seasons can bring a great deal of joy to life. Planting, watering and raking leaves may be a healthy alternative to spending time on an indoor exercise machine, producing a beautiful landscape in addition to muscle tone.

We have many different climates in our country and these vary not only from state to state, but from one community to another. With various climates come different temperatures, rainfall, humidity and amounts of sunlight. There are also different types of soil to consider. Each plant has its own special characteristics and its own needs for water, sunlight and fertilizer. When they receive these in adequate amounts, at appropriate times, they will thrive.

Trees not only add grace to the appearance of a house, they also provide shade and constantly changing shadow patterns. Their roots can help prevent soil erosion. Some provide us with delicious fruit, berries and nuts. Deciduous trees admit winter sunlight and block the summer sun, helping to lower fuel bills. The leaves of some varieties turn beautiful colors in the fall. Evergreens retain their foliage year-round and can be useful as windblocks. They also have a wonderful aroma. Trees and shrubs can provide privacy and dampen noise from busy streets. They attract birds, many of which devour bothersome insects. They will enhance good architecture. They can also be used to hide poor architecture.

This formal garden is contained by a pergola and retaining walls.

Trees are wonderful things for children to climb, and many of us learned a lesson in life from scrapes or even a broken limb when we experienced the inevitability of gravity. When I designed a home for the Kessler family in Maplewood, New Jersey, they asked me to include a treehouse for the children. There was a stair for them to climb and a firefighter's pole for a fast exit. The children liked to sleep there overnight and encouraged their father to join them.

The most important consideration when landscaping around a home is to integrate the landscape scheme with the design of the home

and the neighborhood. The landscaping should carefully consider the layout of the house and the orientation of individual rooms.

Landscaping should be much more than a few token bushes around the base of a house. It is an opportunity to soften the hard lines of a building, to blend a home into its environment, and to add charm to the circumstance through changing colors and patterns.

Unfortunately, there is no such thing as a maintenance-free plant. Cacti need little care, but are only appropriate to desert climes. Deciduous trees may provide stunning colors in the fall but they also involve the need to rake up dead leaves. Trees planted too close to your house might drop leaves on the roof which clog up gutters. They might also drop branches on your roof in a storm. Tree roots can work their way into a sewage line. Nevertheless, a tree adjacent to your house can be a beautiful and symbiotic relationship.

Evergreens have a more compact shape and if planted near a house can look stiff and regimented. The canopy-shaped tree is a most graceful complement to a house. Since appropriate varieties of trees and shrubs vary according to climate and geography, it is best to consult your local nursery for advice. Be sure you are aware of the mature size of any tree you plant. Don't select trees that grow so tall that they throw your house out of scale. A tree that is eighty feet high does not belong next to a single-story home.

A flush curb of concrete or brick will facilitate mowing.

Apple, pear, plum or cherry trees will bring the beneficence of spring blossoms and fresh fruit.

Underground irrigation systems can deliver water (and fertilizer) directly to plants and can be controlled by time clocks to deliver at specified times. Drip or bubbler heads are used for plants and trees, sprinkler heads for lawns. Remember that overwatering is as bad as underwatering.

Depending on the size of your lot, landscaping may include many other possibilities: earth forms — mounds and berms, rocks and boulders; water features — from swimming pools to ponds, fountains and waterfalls; lawns and ground covers, flower gardens, rock gardens, children's play areas, pergolas, trellises, patios, barbecue and picnic areas.

In many developments we see an extravagant use of water — lakes, waterfalls and fountains — that use huge amounts of groundwater to create an image. In desert communities, this device is used to attract potential buyers who come from cooler climates. By creating the effect of an oasis in the desert, developers believe they will increase sales. If we look to the future, the underground water tables in many communities are being drawn down faster than nature is able to replenish them. As the population in many "sunshine

My informal garden.

communities" continues to increase at a rapid rate, we are creating a potential problem for future generations.

If you live in the northern part of the country and look down from an airplane at communities in the Phoenix area, you may be astonished at the number of homes that have a swimming pool in the backyard. Here the swimming pool is the focus of the landscaping scheme and there are fewer lawns. Pools and water features no longer need to take a traditional shape but can be almost any configuration imaginable. Pool finishes include "Pebbletec" or "Hydrazzo," tiny pebbles in a matrix that looks more natural and are more durable than traditional plaster.

There are many options for pool deck surfaces — Saltillo tile, flagstone, slate and granite. The negative edge is a dramatic effect, with water flowing over the edge of the pool to form a seamless transition with the sky. Cleaning is much easier with new equipment that cleans an entire pool every thirty minutes, but if you are planning on a pool, be prepared for lots of maintenance.

A garden is a good way to teach children about the miracle of life.

The most thoughtful type of landscaping in arid climates is xeriscape, meaning using little or no water. Xeriscape is being used for most of the street medians and areas that cities have to maintain. Golf courses are using it for all areas except the target zones and greens. Many homeowners are using it for their front yards. "No-water" landscapes can be designed to be quite attractive, and certainly look more in harmony with the desert environment.

A weed is a wildflower that hasn't been appreciated yet.
　　　　　　　　　　　　　　　　　—Ralph Waldo Emerson

MAINTENANCE

If you foolishly ignore beauty, your life will be impoverished.

—FLLW

Clients were sometimes astonished to arrive and find Mr. Wright, broom in hand, sweeping up dead leaves. He always took care of what he created. He came upon me one day, using a broom so vigorously that a cloud of dust hung in the air.

"Let me show you how to sweep, John," he said kindly, and took the broom from my hands. "Hold it at an angle so that you sweep down, not up. Then you won't fill the air with dirt."

He believed that in order to learn to design architecture that is truly sensitive to the continual need for maintenance, an architect should have hands-on experience. So in the educational program at Taliesin, apprentices are assigned to maintain some part of the buildings and grounds as a seasonal maintenance task. They learn to sweep floors, wash windows, repair roofs and install plumbing — all the many tasks that are part of keeping a building functioning. This experience is in our bones as we design a home.

When a family moves into a home it assumes the responsibility for its upkeep. An architect may design their house in a few months but the family will have to look after it for many years. So it should be obligatory for an architect to design a home that makes maintenance tasks a little easier.

We might all like to have a home that requires no upkeep but there is no such thing. There is, however, the possibility of creating a home that is designed to be easy to maintain. Low-maintenance

Opposite: Sheepherder tent — my first abode at Taliesin.

Below: My bachelor pad.

My apartment today.

Right: *An architect's home is an opportunity to experiment.*

possibilities start in the design process — with the way a home is laid out, the selection of materials used, and the type of mechanical equipment used.

Designing for minimal upkeep includes several basic steps. The first one has to do with what it takes to keep our home clean. The second is what it takes to keep everything operating smoothly. The third is keeping weather out, and the fourth is what it takes to replace or upgrade worn-out items.

I learned a lesson in maintenance when my first house was being built. The house was built in New Jersey by Tom Pampalone, an excellent builder with a fine reputation. When I first met him, he drove me through the neighborhood, pointing out various houses he had built over the years. Suddenly he pulled over to the curb and got out. Taking a ladder out of the back of his truck, he carried it over to a house, leaned it against the wall and proceeded to climb. He had noticed some marks on the wall indicating the gutter had overflowed. He cleaned some dead leaves out of the roof drain and then came back down. He didn't bother to explain. This particular house, it turned out, was thirty years old. It even had a different owner. Tom's son told me later that his father regarded all the houses he built in his lifetime as his children.

I feel the same way about what I design.

The ability to easily clean a home depends on how thoughtfully the basic floor plan is laid out. If the plan includes lots of halls and corridors, there will be more areas to clean. Some materials, especially fabrics and wood, may require special treatment to prevent them from fading in direct sunlight, thus adding to maintenance time. Some materials are easier to clean than others are. If there are lots of spaces that are hard to reach, cleaning will take longer. Kitchens and bathrooms especially should be designed for easy upkeep.

No gutters or downspouts to get clogged up with leaves.

An effective air filter in your air conditioning system (as described in "Environmental Systems") will go a long way towards keeping your home clean by reducing the amount of dust and other airborne particles.

With all our concern over physical fitness, we might sometimes consider using a broom or vacuum cleaner rather than jumping on an exercise machine. Participating in the cleaning of a house adds to our sense of pride in our home and is a good way to get the family doing something constructive together. Children should be taught to regard it as fun and not just a menial chore.

There are central vacuum cleaning systems (which are built into the house framing) but they are not recommended for a moderate-cost home. Outdoors, a leaf blower may seem useful, but it doesn't pick anything up, just redistributes leaves and dust.

Frank Lloyd Wright always had maintenance in mind as he put pencil to paper. His design innovations include the wall-hung flush toilet, outward-sloping self-cleaning glass, and cabinets with a recessed toespace. At the entrance to the Guggenheim Museum, he provided a floor grill that sucked the dust off people's feet before they entered the building.

Architecture today is more maintenance-free than it was in the past. We have simplified surfaces and done away with unnecessary decorative trim. We have mostly done away with gutters and downspouts that can clog up. Cantilevered roofs provide generous overhangs and let the rain that washes the dirt off the roof fall clear of the house. We use fewer painted surfaces and have replaced them with materials that need no paint. With the high cost of home repairs today, savings can be achieved whenever we can do simple tasks ourselves.

Below: A 2,500 sq. ft. three-bedroom home.

Bottom: Low maintenance possibilities start during the design process.

Wright usually eliminated two things from his modest-cost houses: the basement and the attic. His reasoning was that the basement is often relatively expensive to build because it requires excavation, possibly dampproofing. After some years it becomes moldy, dusty and unhealthy. A family tends to throw things down there and then forget about them. (In areas that are subject to tornadoes, however, a basement may serve as a storm cellar.)

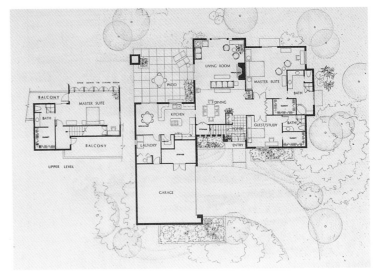

There was a partial basement under one of the wings of Wright's home in Wisconsin. It dated from the time Taliesin was first built, in 1911, and was seldom used. One day Mr. Wright led some of us down there to take a look. We brushed aside the black widow spiders but made a hasty retreat when we discovered a family of skunks had moved in.

Attics also tend to be dusty places. Unless the attic floor is properly designed, it may not be able to carry the accumulated weight of stored materials. Piles of books and magazines can grow to a level never considered by the builder. If the roof has a small leak and the paper gets wet, the load can cause a ceiling to collapse.

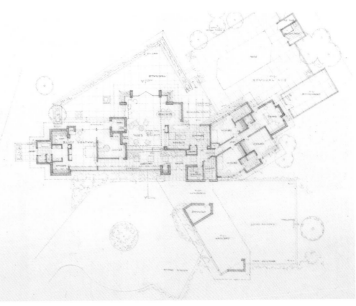

Instead of using basements and attics for storage, I suggest you consider providing more convenient reach-in storage spaces at ground level.

Cleaning your house while your kids are still growing is like shoveling the walk before it stops snowing.
—Phyllis Diller

PRIVACY, SECURITY, SAFETY

Everything has been figured out except how to live.

— Jean-Paul Sartre

PRIVACY

The age of technology redefined our ideas about privacy. Now we have Space Age imaging — the Ikonos satellite can define an object three feet square from over 400 miles away. We also know that almost all forms of electronic communications can be monitored. To counteract this, all sorts of complicated encryption devices are employed. How far we have come in the 150 years since Thoreau lived in a tiny house by Walden Pond and wrote about nature and the simple life!

A gate can define a private area.

In the moderate-size house, built in the suburbs or the country, privacy has to do mostly with views and sound. If your lot is small, less than half an acre, you need to create a sense of privacy without making you feel like you have built your own prison.

Although it is wonderful to live in a home that has a feeling of open space, with an almost seamless connection between indoors and outdoors, this does not imply that you will want to live in a glass box. At the same time that certain views out of your house are desirable, it is necessary to control the views into your house, especially from the street or neighbors. This is all part of the sense of shelter that is the essence of a home; in this case we need shelter from undesirable views.

In some areas of your home, privacy is essential. When we study a site plan, or layout of the lot, we make an assessment of the view possibilities. In this analysis we identify the views we want to see from inside the house, and also the views we want to screen out. Most people

The first step towards privacy is not to open the house to the street.

don't want to look at the house next door. This seems obvious, yet many houses are built without taking it into consideration. Consequently, the inhabitants live with the blinds or curtains closed most of the time. When lot widths are narrow, placing the living area so it faces the street usually means that the space will not be used much.

A view to the outdoors is more important in some rooms than others. The living and dining areas should take first priority when it comes to views. A view from the kitchen may be important to the person cooking. A view from bedrooms is desirable but might have to take second place. Bathrooms usually need light and ventilation but not views, and some spaces, such as garages, closets and storage areas, can be used to block views in. In the layout of the 1997 Life Dream House, I set the kitchen in the center of the house but provided views to the outdoors across the dining area.

Sometimes we build screen walls, six or seven feet high, that block out views but allow the flow of open space above. At times these screen walls may be wood grilles or translucent screens, perhaps with carved wood or art glass patterns. Sometimes we use a closet, such as the coat closet or a reach-in wardrobe, as a visual screen to separate one space from another. These space-dividers allow the free and open flow of space and can help make a small house seem quite spacious.

All homes need a combination of individual space and communal space. The way that the plan of your home is laid out should consider both types, and it should also establish which areas need privacy and which areas do not. If a suburban lot is large enough, one solution is to plan the home around a central garden court. The house need not wrap all sides of the court, but can have rooms on two or more sides, and be enclosed on the other side by a screen wall.

The areas that need the most privacy are the bathrooms. Within the bathroom some parts need even more privacy.

Bedrooms need a degree of privacy. Parents will want infants to be close, but as children grow up, there is a need for space separation. That is when most parents want their bedroom to have some degree of isolation from the children, and when children will want their own space.

One way to achieve this is to put the parents' on one side of the house and the children on the other side. A room near the master bedroom can serve as a nursery. After it is no longer needed for that purpose it can be converted to another use. Separating the children's rooms from the parents' quarters can help bring harmony to family life.

Locating closets and storage areas on the walls between bedrooms is an excellent way to control noise.

SECURITY
Home security systems and services deal with break-ins, burglary, fire alarms and medical

Each bedroom has its own garden patio, screened by a six-foot-high wall.

emergencies. There are many types of systems available. Most of them utilize sophisticated electronic monitoring devices. These include motion detectors, sensors that ascertain when a window or door is opened, closed circuit TV (CCTV) cameras, and so forth.

A combination motion detector and photoelectric cell is a simple and affordable device that can be mounted on the outside of your house. As you walk past it after dark it will turn on a light for a few minutes. This not only helps a homeowner find their way at night but also acts as a deterrent to prowlers.

If you have small children and a swimming pool, you should consider getting a pool alarm to alert you if a child (or pet) falls in the pool.

Another benefit in having an efficient home security system is that it will reduce the premiums on your homeowners' insurance.

SAFETY

Safety in the home is an issue that doesn't get the attention it deserves and statistics back this up. Every day in the United States there are 50,000 accidents. The home is often the place where they occur. In many cases this can be attributed to poor design of the house or its components. Age has a significant impact on the chance of a mishap and the youngest and oldest are the most prone.

A high, step-over threshold at the front door is a hazard, an invitation for a fall. A low-profile interlocking threshold, less than an inch high, is much safer. Your front door should

High windows admit light but not public view.

Opposite: *Pools should have a safety alarm that sounds if a child falls in.*

Privacy achieved by landscaping.

A detached guest cottage offers privacy.

always be sheltered from the weather. A deep roof overhang at the entry will keep rain, snow, ice, sun and wind away from your door.

As mentioned earlier, a single step can create a tripping hazard, so I never include one in my designs. If a small change in level is needed, I use at least three steps or a shallow ramp. Outdoors I use steps with sixteen-inch-wide treads and a four-inch riser. These take up more area but are much easier to walk up, especially for the physically challenged, older people, children and pets. Sometimes I use a ramp instead of stairs to create a flow of space continuity.

Be cautious about slippery floor surfaces, especially if they can get wet. Polished marble may look nice but it is slippery when wet. As for loose carpets on slick floors, they are an accident waiting to happen.

A smoke alarm could save your life. All building codes require them. The two major types are ionization and photoelectric. They need not be expensive — some higher rated brands detect

Below: A walled garden court at the entrance affords privacy.

Below right: The central garden courtyard is a way to create a secluded area.

both smoke and flames and cost under thirty dollars. There are also systems where alarms trigger each other. Essential locations are the kitchen and bedrooms. You should also have one at the top of stairs and in a basement if you have one.

You have a big investment in your home and a much bigger one in human life, so be prepared. Your family should stage a rehearsal of what to do in case of an emergency. Children should be familiar with how to get out of their bedrooms, which should have windows that are accessible and large enough for them to climb out of.

According to the National Fire Protection Association, there are some 40,000 house fires and 350 deaths a year attributable to electrical problems. One third of the ninety million homes in the U.S. are over fifty years old. Most have some faulty wiring and their electrical systems do not meet minimum safety standards. With only a few ungrounded outlets per room, homeowners rely on extension cords.

You should have GFCI (ground fault circuit interrupter) outlets in bathrooms and kitchens. AFCIs (arc fault circuit interrupters) installed in circuit breaker panels use microprocessor technology to detect potential wiring problems. Overloaded circuits, loose electrical connections and damaged insulation are often the culprits. Ask a reputable electrician for an estimate to make an inspection.

If you want information on a product, the U.S. Consumer Product Safety Commission (CPSC) can assist.

An ounce of prevention is worth a pound of cure.

— Old adage

Top: *A home needs both individual and communal space.*

Above: *You will feel more secure if your home opens to the rear, not the street.*

THE REGULATORY PROCESS

I love being a writer. What I can't stand is the paperwork.

— Peter De Vries

In a documentary titled, "The Real Cost of Regulation," John Stossel, investigative reporter for *ABC News,* points out, "The damage done by regulation is so vast, it's often hard to see. The money wasted consists not only of the taxes taken directly from us to pay for bureaucrats, but also for the lost energy that goes into filling out the forms. Then there's the distraction of creative power. Many of the smartest people in the country go into law. This doesn't create a richer, freer society. Nor do regulations only depress the economy. They depress the spirit. What's happened to America? Why do we allow government to make decisions for us as if we were children? In a free society we should be allowed to take risks and learn from them. What makes America thrive isn't regulation, it's freedom."

If everybody in the building industry were competent, diligent and scrupulously honest, there would be little need for building codes and regulations. Since mankind has not reached such a state of perfection, and probably never will, we must rely on laws and enforcement methods to ensure the health and safety of our buildings. So we have developed building codes to specify the strength of building materials and formulas for the design of structural members and systems.

The regulatory process today is extremely complex. To begin with, there are several layers: federal, regional, state, county and city. Each jurisdiction has its own laws, zoning and building codes. On top of these, individual housing developments and communities usually have their own design and construction guidelines. These laws and codes are most complicated, hard to interpret and sometimes contradictory. They are also subject to amendments. Did you

"What makes America thrive isn't regulation, it's freedom."

know that China, with a population of over two billion people, has fewer lawyers than the city of New York?

Many architectural and legal firms now have members who specialize in zoning and building regulations. The purpose of zoning laws is to establish allowable uses, prohibiting and restricting certain types. They set minimum lot sizes and maximum building coverage. They describe building setbacks from the front, sides and rear property lines. They specify required open space, maximum heights for buildings, requirements for parking, landscaping and signage and set forth a process for submittals and reviews.

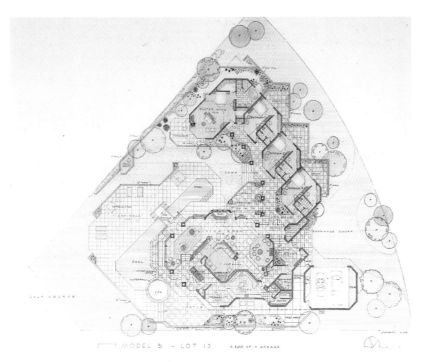

Building codes describe approved types of construction and set minimum standards for structural design, ceiling heights, stairs, sanitation, ventilation, natural light, exits and fire alarm systems. Many communities have adopted the Uniform Building Code — a move in the right direction.

Houses must be strong enough to resist the forces of gravity, wind, water, sun, freezing and sometimes seismic activity. We must take into account the types and conditions of soil underneath footings.

People and property need protection from fire and smoke. The quality of air in buildings must be a concern. Electrical

Above: *Each bedroom has two exits.*

In a free society we should be allowed to take risks and learn from them.

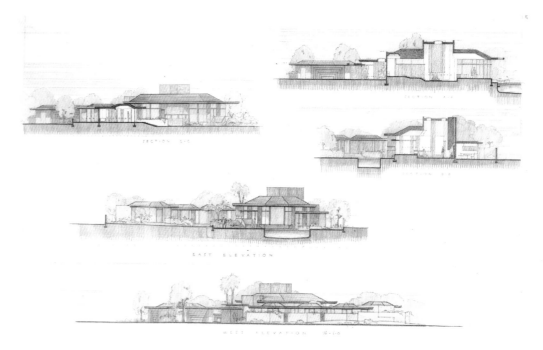

systems must be designed and installed so as not to give shocks or start fires. We must antic-
ipate panic and be sure there are ways for people to exit safely during moments of crisis.
There must be ways for people with disabilities to have access and egress. We must be sure
that there is adequate parking available and that emergency vehicles can be accommodated.

All architects and builders have a responsibility to human health and safety. Homes must
be adequately lit, with a sufficient amount of fresh, conditioned air.

*Regulations should not
stifle creativity.*

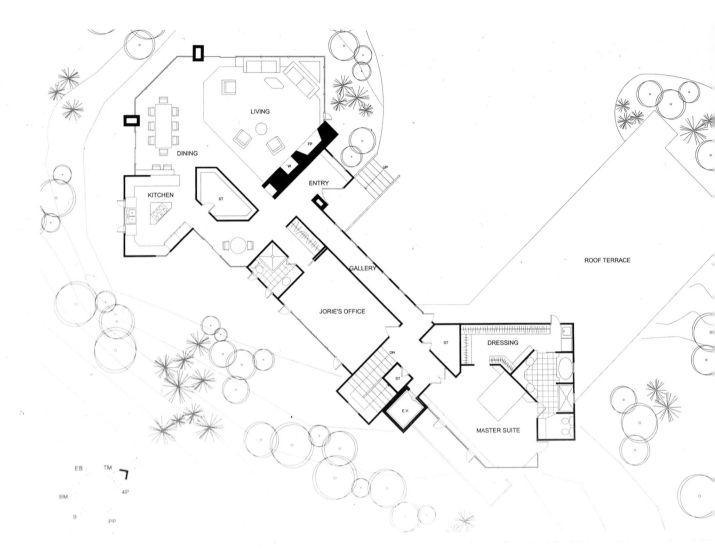

The following labels appear in the floor plan:

LIVING

DINING

KITCHEN

ENTRY

GALLERY

JORIE'S OFFICE

DRESSING

ROOF TERRACE

MASTER SUITE

If you are building a home, quite obviously you should not try to hide anything from, or antagonize, building inspectors. If they think you and your builder are cooperative they are usually more reasonable when they decide whether a detail meets code requirements.

A basic problem with the regulatory system is also found in the field of education. There is an old saying that those who can, do; those who can't, teach. This is somewhat unfair, since most teachers are hard-working individuals dedicated to an essential cause. Many work in other professions when they are not teaching. But it does point out the gap between hands-on experience and intellectual theory. The individuals who work for governmental agencies have to struggle with the fact that they are regulating, not doing. The nature of their work tends to be less exciting than designing or building, yet it affords a certain sense of power, since these people have the authority to approve or disapprove the work of professionals.

Every once in a while we deal with an enlightened building official who is dedicated to ensuring that a building is structurally sound, safe and healthy. These people work with us, recognizing that we share the same goals. We are both looking for the best and safest solution.

Most architectural schools do not devote enough time to the study of building codes. When a young architect, diploma in hand, sets foot into the business world, a shock usually awaits him as he submits his first set of plans for a building permit. The many different codes, laws, regulations, design guidelines and the complicated approval process quickly shatter the dream that architects just design buildings.

Most regulations are written as proscriptive, that is, all they tell us are the things that we cannot do. I think that in the future more thought should be given to establishing positive descriptions of designs and procedures that do meet regulations, with examples of things that designers and builders can and should do.

To understand something, most people look for examples. I would like to see, for instance, a demonstration model house built in every community. The model would include not only examples of the things that don't work and are not allowed, but also examples of good solutions to the problems of human health and safety.

All else passes. Art alone, enduring, stays with us.

—Theophile Gautier

Regulations should include exemplary solutions to public health and safety.

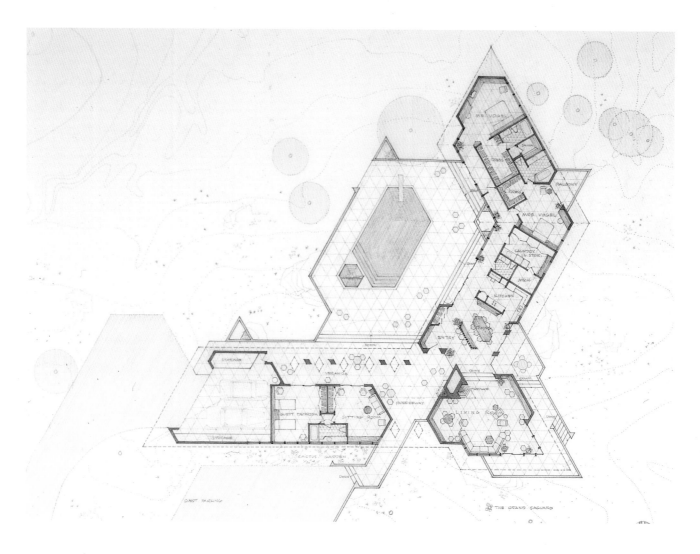

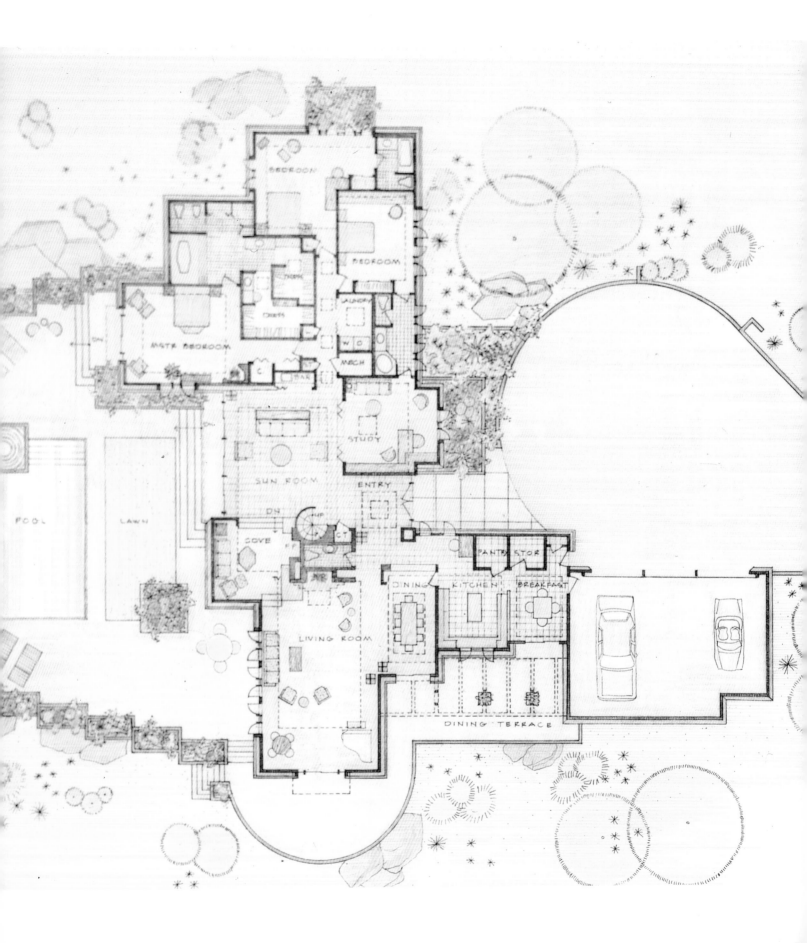

BEDROOM

BEDROOM

MSTR BEDROOM

STUDY

SUN ROOM

ENTRY

POOL

LAWN

COVE

LIVING ROOM

DINING

KITCHEN

BREAKFAST

PANTRY STOR

DINING TERRACE

A VISION FOR THE FUTURE

My interest is in the future because I am going to spend the rest of my life there.

— Charles F. Kettering

There is a time and place for everything. The housing industry, like a slumbering giant, is slowly waking up. If we are ever to raise the level of design of the homes in which we live, now is the time and America is the place. We need to apply to our dwellings the skills that produced the automobile, the airplane, television and the computer. We need to integrate art, science and religion.

When we think about the future, most people's minds immediately turn to technology. We ask questions like, "Will computers be smarter than people? Will nanotechnolgy develop robots that can do anything? What will replace the Internet? Will our cars run on autopilot?" Even the smartest people sometimes have trouble seeing into the future. "I think there is a world market for maybe five computers," said Thomas Watson, the chairman of IBM in 1943. And in 1981, Bill Gates asked, "Who in their right mind would want more than 640K of RAM?"

It will not be enough to rely only on science and technology. Frank Lloyd Wright reminded us that our house becomes more of a home by being a work of art. We should take this to heart. Our home is a significant financial investment, one that is for the most part incapable of being moved around. We cannot produce new models every few years and trade them in or throw them away, the way we do our cars, TV sets and telephones. We should pay more attention to creating a home that is functional, durable and timeless in its beauty. Our home will have a profound effect on the quality of our lives and the well-being of our children.

"We are without a philosophy now to meet those changes which are inevitable and

The significance of the individual home as a democratic unit.

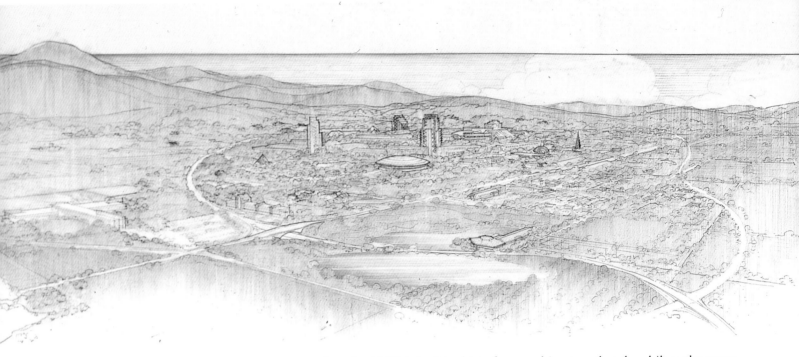

Chayeh — a plan for a model city in Arizona.

occurring everywhere," said Wright. "And it is from architecture that the philosophy must come. Anything that increases the potency, the significance, and the value of the individual home as a democratic unit will make it richer, more pleasant to live in."

The first step in giving everybody a better home will come by way of education. Until we enlighten society about architecture, and teach our next generation to appreciate and demand higher quality in the design and construction of their homes, we will just continue to travel the same circular road that leads to nowhere. If we are honest about it, when we drive through suburbia we are not confronted with man-made beauty. If we want beauty there we must hope that someone has planted trees or flowers. The occasional open space is like taking a breath of fresh air. But it doesn't have to be this way.

Until homeowners start to demand innovation, builders will continue to offer up the same stale goods that they have for years. In this market-driven economy, as long as the seller can make a nice profit without needing to change the product, there is little incentive to innovate and improve residential design.

When it comes to predicting the future, some have had a clear vision while others have had

View of Wright's idea for Broadacre City.

a more obscured view. The Greek philosopher Heraclitus declared, "There is only one thing mankind can be certain of and that is that everything is in the process of change." (For this piece of wisdom, the citizens of Athens promptly stoned him to death.)

In order to vitalize our society, we must constantly renew our ideas and efforts. In times of prosperity, affluence can be a greater challenge than adversity. This age of instant information has

218

brought us to the point where we know everything about the past twenty-four hours but much less about the past twenty-four years.

My own vision for the home of the future, assuredly optimistic, starts with the quality of space. The space of the neighborhood environment, the space between houses and the sense of spaciousness within a home.

I believe that we will become more and more appreciative of the effect that a beautiful environment can have on our life. We will realize that a house in the Arizona desert should be appropriate to that arid environment, while a house in Michigan should relate to its northern climate. If you exchanged the two houses you would immediately know they were inappropriate. Houses will be a grace to the landscape, not a disgrace. We will see fewer box-shaped houses. As people become more aware of what constitutes good design in a home they will insist on a higher standard. The circular form, which is more natural and humanistic than the rectangle, will become prevalent.

Cities should be as beautiful by day as at night.

Our home will represent the spirit of freedom so essential to democracy. It will be designed to link indoors and outdoors and to utilize natural daylight. We will light, heat and cool our homes using far less energy than we do today.

Will houses in the future be different because we have learned to control the weather? According to the scientists, the weather will be uncontrollable for the foreseeable future, so don't count on that.

How will our home relate to the global environment? Several years ago an expensive experiment was conducted in southern Arizona. An enormous glass and concrete habitat called Biosphere II was erected and filled with everything deemed necessary for the balance of life — trees, crops, water, air and eight humans. The building was sealed tight and over a period of two years was supposed to demonstrate how we could engineer a sustainable ecosystem. But before the two years were up the seal had to be broken because oxygen levels fell severely and the rise of nitrous oxide levels threatened brain damage. What the Biosphere did

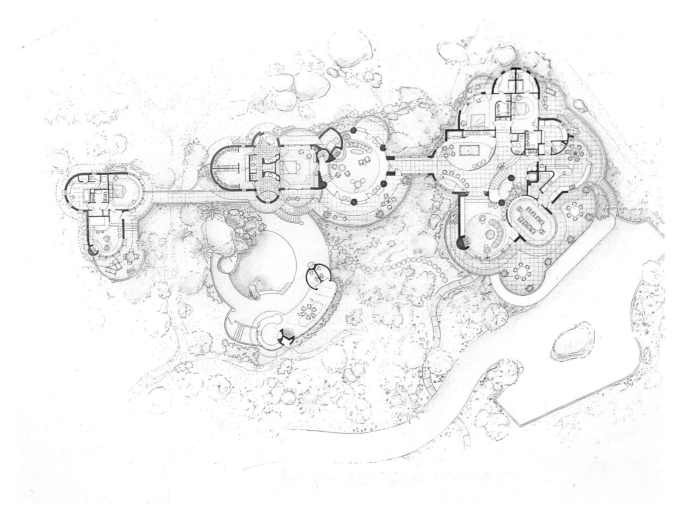

prove was that humans cannot devise life-supporting systems that match Nature's ecosystems. So we must learn to protect Nature.

Other experiments have shown the importance of biodiversity — ecosystems that have many different species are the best for plant growth and are more resistant to drought and soil degradation.

Significant improvements are being made in America. We are starting to reduce air- and water-born pollutants. There is an increased sense of awareness of our responsibility to preserve the quality of our environment, though we have not yet advanced to the point of living up to the ancient Native American wisdom of planning ahead for seven generations.

We are slowly learning to respect this earth — it offers us such amazing gifts. We are realizing it is possible to build without destroying the environment. In our struggle to connect with nature we find ourselves in a strange position, because it would seem that Nature doesn't care much about us. Although we can't live without Nature, Nature doesn't seem to need us. If all the people were to go away, it would get along just fine. Humans are a part of Nature, so if we do not treat it with honor, we are dishonoring ourselves.

A sense of global integrity is a difficult thing for many people to comprehend. Anything of this scale can be mind-numbing, like looking at the Milky Way and trying to imagine its size.

I believe that the way to approach our contribution to the future of the world, to the creation of a better environment, is to start with our home. This is something of a scale we can understand. It is a circumstance that we can embrace, where we can make a difference.

Our home affects the quality of our lives and our children's lives.

The home of the future no doubt will have some interesting technological features. We can extrapolate from what's available today to make fairly safe predictions: We will be awakened by our computer to the sound of our favorite music. As we enter the bathroom we will be scanned for our weight and state of health. While we wash, a list of our day's activities will be displayed on the bathroom mirror. In the kitchen, breakfast will be automatically prepared with the type of nourishment best suited to our current health and planned activities.

Our house will sense our physical and emotional states and change the colors of the walls to either energize or calm us. Since the interior walls of our future home are formed with electronic space screens, our house will be smaller. When an interior wall is not needed, it can be made to disappear. We will be able to instantly change an opaque wall into one that is translucent or transparent. Walls will have an ever-changing display of world-famous art. Our homes will have realistic holographic sculptures that can also be changed at whim.

Most of us will have the option of working at home or the office, because everything will be electronically linked. As we become more and more lazy from having so many things done for us, we will need to take more time in our exercise room. As we exercise on a machine, thanks to virtual reality we will feel as though we are riding a bike in the mountains of Colorado or running down a beach in Hawaii. In addition to surrounding each member of the family with appropriate colors and light levels, our home will provide optimal temperature and humidity controls for each individual.

There are some amazing possibilities ahead for powering the automobile and eventually

Homes should complement the magical and beautiful world in which we live.

our home. Fuel cell technology, for instance, combines hydrogen and oxygen to produce electricity without combustion. When this is perfected it will contribute to a healthier planet and conserve our natural resources.

Technology will never solve all the problems of the world or make our lives perfect. But, despite wars and man-made tragedies, some aspects of America are encouraging. We are largely a nation of "volunteers," willing to give freely of our time, knowledge and resources. We admire the entrepreneurial spirit and encourage young people to show initiative. I believe we will, in time, pass through the litigious climate that currently has us in its grip. Each one of us can make a difference. As an architect, I believe I have been given an opportunity to help make the world a better place in which to live. Working together, homeowners, architects, engineers and builders can create homes that are responsible to our shared environment; homes that are in harmony with Nature, in human scale and complementary to the beautiful and magical world in which we live. Then our homes will be a heritage that we will be proud to leave to our children.

Faith in democracy — Walt Whitman's "And thou, America…".

Learn from yesterday, live for today, hope for tomorrow.

—Anonymous

222

APPENDIX

RESIDENTIAL PROJECTS

Single Family Residences
Anderson Residence, Las Vegas, NV
Beesley Residence, Salt Lake City, UT
Betz Residence, Scottsdale, AZ
Brandfass Residence, Cave Creek, AZ
Brown, L. Residence, Phoenix, AZ
Fields Residence, Phoenix, AZ
Flagg Residence, San Luis Obispo, CA
Francis Residence, Redding, CA
Gaddis Residence, Park City, UT
Gangemi Residence, Scottsdale, AZ
Garner, J. Residence, Gold Mountain, CA
Gehring Residence, Whitehaven, FL
Green Residence, Scottsdale, AZ
Haskins Residence, Larkspur, CO
Holm Residence, Duck, NC
Ingersoll Residence, Scottsdale, AZ *
Jackson Residence, Paradise Valley, AZ
Kessler Residence, Maplewood, NJ
Kuhnley Residence, Scottsdale, AZ
Legler Residence, Scottsdale, Arizona
Life Dream House at Gold Mountain, CA
Luce Cottage, Phoenix, AZ
Lykes/Melton Residence, Phoenix, AZ
Maas Residence, Scottsdale, AZ
Main Residence, San Luis Obispo, CA
McRae Residence, Jackson, WY
Middleton Residence, Scottsdale, AZ
Murphy Residence, Scottsdale, AZ
Myers Residence, Scottsdale, AZ *
Payne Residence, Carefree, AZ

Residence for a Royal Family, Saudi Arabia
Satin Residence, Scottsdale, AZ
Shostak Residence, San Tan Mtns, AZ
Silvern Residence, Phoenix, AZ
Simon Residence 1, Summerlin, NV
Simon Residence 2, Summerlin, NV
Snow Residence, Fountain Hills, AZ
Strother Residence, Rancho Mirage, CA
Theilen Residence, Dallas, TX
Ullman Residence, Scottsdale, AZ
Westphal Residence, Carefree, AZ
York Residence, Scottsdale, AZ

F LL Wright Designs (built after 1959)
Sims Residence, Kamuela, HI
Baumgarten Residence, Pauling, NY
West Residence, Occaquaan, VA
McBroom Residence, Warren County, VA

Model Houses
Prototype House for the Sonoran Desert, AZ
Sunstream, Desert Springs, CA
Sunsprite, Desert Springs, CA
Model House for Taliesin Gates, Scottsdale, AZ
Three Prototype Houses for California City
Prototype House for Cochiti Lake, NM
Prototype House for Colorado City, CO
Model House for the Mohave Desert, CA
Entrada Model Home, St. George, UT

Production Housing

Mountain View Estates, Paradise Valley, AZ

Mountain View East, Paradise Valley, AZ

Ranch House models A, B and C for the National
   Homes Corp.

Mobile Home Designs for National Homes Corp.

Mobile Home Designs for International Homes Corp.

Lightweight Concrete House Prototype, AZ

Prefab house for an American Family

Cottages and Casitas

Lykes Summer Cottage, Tuxedo, NC

Hillside Villas at Desert Highlands, Scottsdale, AZ

Golf Casitas, Scottsdale, AZ

Sedona Resort Cottages, Sedona, AZ

Oceanside Casitas, Belize

Boulders Casitas, Carefree, AZ

Hospitality Casita, Scottsdale, AZ

Quadruplex Housing Unit, Scottsdale, AZ

Schoch Ski Cabin, New Market, VA

Canoe Bay Guest Cottages, Chetek, WI

Remodeling & Additions

Olgivanna Lloyd Wright Apartment, Scottsdale, AZ

Rattenbury Residence, Scottsdale, AZ

Dugan Residence Remodeling, Houston, TX

Benton Residence Remodeling, Phoenix, AZ

Cohen Addition to Fields Residence, Phoenix, AZ

McKracken Residence Renovations, Paradise Valley, AZ

Melton Renovations to Lykes Residence, Phoenix, AZ

Tracy Residence Addition, Seattle, WA

Kelly Residence Remodel, Phoenix, AZ

Legler Residence Addition, Scottsdale, AZ

Ravenswood Residence Remodel, Phoenix, AZ

Cottages Remodel, Arizona Biltmore, Phoenix, AZ

Thompson Residence Remodel, Adelaide, Australia

Multi-Family Housing

Mountain Run Apartments, New Market, VA

Colorado Biltmore Condominiums, Denver, CO

Pine Tree Apartments, Madison, WI

Harbortown Inn Timeshare Units, Ventura, CA

Residential Master Plans

Acacia Community, Mesa, AZ

Desert Highlands, Scottsdale, AZ

Desert Mountain, Scottsdale, AZ

Waikapu Valley Estates, Maui, HI

South Kohala Estates, Waimea, HI

Entrada at Snow Canyon, St. George, UT

Isleton Community, Isleton, CA

Mountain Run, New Market, VA

Taliesin Gates, Scottsdale, AZ

Ancala West, Scottsdale, AZ

Deerfield, Lehi, UT

Brookbank, Heber, AZ

Reef Colony, Ambergris Caye, Belize

Spanish Reef, Ambergris Caye, Belize

Corrigan-Marley Properties, Scottsdale, AZ

Greer Ranch, Murrieta, CA *

Murrieta Oaks, Murrieta, CA *

Hawksnest, Carefree, AZ *

Bool Residential Community, Scottsdale, AZ

McDowell Mountain Ranch. Scottsdale, AZ

Casitas Del Solar, Tucson, AZ

Millennium Master Plan, Paloma Ranch, AZ

Scottsdale Highlands, Scottsdale, AZ

Rockwood Canyon, San Diego, CA *

Saddleback Mountain, Scottsdale, AZ

McDowell Mountain Ranch, Scottsdale, AZ

Mesa Del Rio, Hesperia, CA

Moreno Valley Project, Moreno Valley, CA

Deerfield, Lehi, UT

Desert Enclave, Cave Creek, AZ

Whetstone Ranch, Benson, AZ *

Whetstone Springs Village, Benson, AZ *

Silver Sun, Dunellon, FL

Castle Hill, Christchurch, New Zealand

In association with Gerry Jones

THE 1997 LIFE DREAM HOUSE

An affordable way to get an architect-designed home is to purchase a set of plans. Several different plan variations and roof configurations of the 1997 Life Dream House are available. The basic model has three bedrooms. Variations include a four-bedroom model and a two-master suite model. The two-story version fits on a smaller lot.

There are five different roof styles: hipped, gable, flat, pyramid and barrel vault.

The house plans may be viewed online at <www.life.com/Life/dreamhouse/taliesin/taliesin.html> Plans can be ordered from:

LIFE Dream House/Home Styles,
P.O Box 75488
St. Paul, MN 55175-0488.

Phone: 1-888-277-5055.

The cost of a set of plans is about $600. The house has been built in most parts of the U.S. at a cost of $200,000 to $400,000 depending on the model, materials, and the part of the country it which it is built.

STRUCTURE OF THE FRANK LLOYD WRIGHT FOUNDATION

The Frank Lloyd Wright Foundation (the parent organization)

The Taliesin Fellowship (the residential community)

Taliesin Architects Archives

The Frank Lloyd Wright School of Architecture (a fully accredited educational institution, NCA and NCARB)

The William Wesley Peters Library

Desert Shelter Program

The Frank Lloyd Wright Archives Licensing Program

The Frank Lloyd Wright Collection

Publications and Exhibitions

Public Education and Access Tour Program and Bookstores (Taliesin and Taliesin West)

Other Programs:

Education Outreach

Taliesin Preservation, Inc.

Development

Taliesin Fellows, Taliesin Journal

Reunions

Affiliated Groups, Associate Members

The Frank Lloyd Wright Building Conservancy

FURTHER READING

Many artists and architects are collectors. I am no exception. I collect works of art, seashells and books. I have tried to gather every book and article written by and about Frank Lloyd Wright. Every year I accumulate more books and articles. To accommodate them, I have built bookshelves in every room. As a consequence, I find myself living in a library.

In 1978, Robert L. Sweeney wrote *Frank Lloyd Wright, An Annotated Bibliography*. It lists 2,095 publications by or about his life and his work. Some are out of print now, but many are available in libraries. New books and articles appear every year.

The following books were my sources of information. An asterisk * denotes my recommendation to those who are planning to build a house.

By Frank Lloyd Wright

An American Architecture. Edited by Edgar Kaufmann. New York: Horizon Press, Architectural Press, 1955.

An Autobiography. London: Faber, Hyperion Press, 1945.

The Complete 1925 "Wendigen" Series. New York: Dover Publications, 1992.

The Disappearing City. New York: William Farquhar Payson, 1932.

Drawings and Plans — The Early Period (1893–1909). New York: Dover Publications, 1983.

Drawings for a Living Architecture. New York: Horizon Press, the Bear Run Foundation Inc, and the Edgar J. Kaufmann Charitable Foundation, 1959.

The Future of Architecture. New York: New American Library, 1970.

Genius and the Mobocracy. New York: Duell, Sloan and Pearce, 1949.

In the Cause of Architecture: Essays by Frank Lloyd Wright for Architectural Record 1908–1952. New York: Architectural Record, 1975.

The Japanese Print: An Interpretation. New York: Horizon Press, 1967.

The Natural House. London: Pitman, 1971.*

Selected Drawings Portfolio. New York and Tokyo: Horizon/ADA, 1957–59.

The Story of the Tower: The Tree that Escaped the Crowded Forest. New York: Horizon Press, 1956.

A Testament. New York: Horizon Press, Architectural Press, 1957.

When Democracy Builds. Chicago: University of Chicago Press, 1945.

Writings and Buildings. Selected by E. Kaufmann and Ben Raeburn. New York: Meridian Books, 1960.*

Hitchcock, Henry Russell, editor. *In the Nature of Materials, 1887–1941: The Buildings of Frank Lloyd Wright*. New York: Duell, Sloan & Pearce, 1942.

Pfeiffer, Bruce Brooks, editor. *Frank Lloyd Wright in the Realm of Ideas*. Carbondale, IL: Southern Illinois University Press, 1988.

———. *Frank Lloyd Wright: Monograph 1887–1901. Vol. 1*. Tokyo: A.D.A. Edita, Tokyo Co., Ltd, 1985.

———. *Frank Lloyd Wright: Monograph 1902–1906. Vol. 2*. Tokyo: A.D.A. Edita, Tokyo Co., Ltd, 1985.

———. *Frank Lloyd Wright: Monograph 1907–1913. Vol. 3*. Tokyo: A.D.A. Edita, Tokyo Co., Ltd, 1985.

———. *Frank Lloyd Wright: Monograph 1914–1923. Vol. 4*. Tokyo: A.D.A. Edita, Tokyo Co., Ltd, 1985.

———. *Frank Lloyd Wright: Monograph 1924–1936. Vol. 5*. Tokyo: A.D.A. Edita, Tokyo Co., Ltd, 1985.

———. *Frank Lloyd Wright: Monograph 1937–1941*. Vol. 6. Tokyo: A.D.A. Edita, 1985.

———. *Frank Lloyd Wright: Monograph 1942–1950*. Vol. 7. Tokyo: A.D.A. Edita, 1985.

———. *Frank Lloyd Wright: Monograph 1951–1959*. Vol. 8. Tokyo: A.D.A. Edita, 1985.

———. *Frank Lloyd Wright: Preliminary Studies 1889–1916*. Vol. 9. Tokyo: A.D.A. Edita, 1985.

———. *Frank Lloyd Wright: Preliminary Studies 1917–1932*. Vol. 10. Tokyo: A.D.A. Edita, 1985.

———. *Frank Lloyd Wright: Preliminary Studies 1933–1959*. Vol. 11. Tokyo: A.D.A. Edita, 1985.

———. *Frank Lloyd Wright: In His Renderings 1887–1959*. Vol. 12. Tokyo: A.D.A. Edita, 1985.

———. *Frank Lloyd Wright Selected Houses. Vol. I Early Houses*. Tokyo: A.D.A. Edita, 1991.

———. *Frank Lloyd Wright Selected Houses. Vol. 2 Taliesin*. Tokyo: A.D.A. Edita, 1990.

———. *Frank Lloyd Wright Selected Houses. Vol. 3 Taliesin West*. Tokyo: A.D.A. Edita, 1989.

———. *Frank Lloyd Wright Selected Houses. Vol. 4 Fallingwater*. Tokyo: A.D.A. Edita, 1990.

———. *Frank Lloyd Wright Selected Houses. Vol. 5. Tokyo:* A.D.A. Edita, 1990.

———. *Frank Lloyd Wright Selected Houses. Vol. 6.* Tokyo: A.D.A. Edita, 1991.

———. *Frank Lloyd Wright Selected Houses. Vol. 7.* Tokyo: A.D.A. Edita, 1991.

———. *Frank Lloyd Wright Selected Houses. Vol. 8 Concrete & Block*. Tokyo: A.D.A. Edita, 1991.

———. *Frank Lloyd Wright: Collected Writings Vol. 1, 1894–1930*. New York: Rizzoli in association with the Frank Lloyd Wright Foundation, 1992.

———. *Frank Lloyd Wright: Collected Writings Vol. 2, 1930–32*. New York: Rizzoli in association with the Frank Lloyd Wright Foundation, 1992.

———. *Frank Lloyd Wright: Collected Writings Vol. 3, 1931–39*. New York: Rizzoli in association with the Frank Lloyd Wright Foundation, 1993.

———. *Frank Lloyd Wright: Collected Writings Vol. 4, 1939–49*. New York: Rizzoli in association with the Frank Lloyd Wright Foundation, 1994.

———. *Frank Lloyd Wright: Collected Writings Vol. 5, 1949–59*. New York: Rizzoli in association with the

Frank Lloyd Wright Foundation, 1995.

———. *Letters to Clients*. Fresno, CA: The Press at California State University, 1986.

———. *Letters to Architects*. Fresno, CA: The Press at California State University, 1984.

———. *Letters to Apprentices*. Fresno, CA: The Press at California State University, 1982.

———. *Frank Lloyd Wright: The Crowning Decade, 1949–59*. Fresno, CA: The Press at California State University, 1989.

———. *The Guggenheim Correspondence*. Carbondale, IL: Southern Illinois University, 1986.

By Olgivanna Lloyd Wright

Frank Lloyd Wright: His Life, His Work, His Words. London: Pitman, 1970.*

Our House. New York: Horizon Press, 1959.

Roots of Life. New York: Horizon Press, 1963.

The Shining Brow. New York: Horizon Press, 1960.

The Struggle Within. New York: Horizon Press, 1955.

By Iovanna Lloyd Wright

Architecture: Man in Possession of His Earth, [with a] Biography. London: Macdonald & Co, 1963.*

By members of the Taliesin Community

Alofsin, Anthony. *Frank Lloyd Wright: The Lost Years, 1910–1922*. Chicago: University of Chicago Press, 1998.

Barney, Maginel Wright. *The Valley of the God-Almighty Joneses*. New York: Appleton-Century, 1965.

Birk, Melanie. *Frank Lloyd Wright's Fifty Views of Japan*. San Francisco: Pomegranate, 1996.

Boulton, Alexander O. *Frank Lloyd Wright, Architect: An Illustrated Biography*. New York: Rizzoli, 1993.

Brierly, Cornelia. *Tales of Taliesin*. San Francisco: Pomegranate, 2000.

Brooks, H. Allen. *The Prairie School: Frank Lloyd Wright and His Midwest Contemporaries*. Toronto: University of Toronto Press, 1972.

———. *Writings on Wright*. Cambridge, MA: MIT Press, 1983.

Constantino, Maria. *Frank Lloyd Wright*. New York: Crescent Books, 1991.

de Fries, H., ed. *Frank Lloyd Wright: Aus dem Lebenswere eines Architekten.* Berlin: Ernst Pollak, 1926.

de Long, David G., ed. *Frank Lloyd Wright and the Living City.* Milan, Italy: Viyra Design Museum, 1998.

Dunham, Judith. *Details of Frank Lloyd Wright: The California Work, 1909–1974.* London: Thames & Hudson, 1994.

Drexler, Arthur, ed. *The Drawings of Frank Lloyd Wright.* New York: Horizon Press, 1962.

Farr, Finis. *Frank Lloyd Wright.* London: J. Cape, 1962.

Gebhard, David. *Romanza: California Architecture of FLLW.* San Francisco: Chronicle Books, 1997.

Grehan, Farrell. *Visions of Wright.* New York: Little, Brown & Co., 1998.

Guerrero, Pedro. *Picturing Wright.* San Francisco: Pomegranate Artbooks, 1993.

Guggenheimer, Tobias. *A Taliesin Legacy: The Architecture of Frank Lloyd Wright's Apprentices.* New York: Van Nostrand Reinhold, 1995.

Gutheim, Frederick, ed. *Frank Lloyd Wright on Architecture: Selected Writings (1894–1940).* New York: Grosset & Dunlap, 1941.

Hanks, David A. *The Decorative Designs of Frank Lloyd Wright.* London: Studio Vista, 1979.

Hart, Spencer. *Frank Lloyd Wright.* New York: Barnes & Noble, 1993.

Heinz, Thomas A. *Frank Lloyd Wright.*

———. *Frank Lloyd Wright: Glass Art.* London: Academy Editions, 1994.

———. *Frank Lloyd Wright: Interiors and Furniture.* London: Academy Editions, 1994.

———. *Frank Lloyd Wright: Field Guide to Metro Chicago.* London: Academy Editions, 1996.

Hoffmann, Donald. *Frank Lloyd Wright: Architecture and Nature.* London: Constable, 1986.

———. *Frank Lloyd Wright's Dana House.* New York: Dover, 1996.

———. *Frank Lloyd Wright's Robie House.* New York: Dover, 1984.

———. *Frank Lloyd Wright's Hollyhock House.* New York: Dover, 1992.

Izzo, Alberto, and Camillo Gubitosi. *Frank Lloyd Wright: Three Quarters of a Century of Drawings.* New York: Horizon Press, 1981.

Jacobs, Herbert, and Katherine Jacobs. *Building with Frank Lloyd Wright.* San Francisco: Chronicle Books, 1978.

James, Cary. *Frank Lloyd Wright's Imperial Hotel.* New York: Dover, 1988.

Johnson, Donald. *Frank Lloyd Wright Versus America: The 1930's.* Cambridge, MA: MIT Press, 1990.

Kaufmann, Edgar. *9 Commentaries on Frank Lloyd Wright.* Cambridge, MA: MIT Press, 1989.

Kruty, Paul. *Frank Lloyd Wright and Midway Gardens.* Urbana and Chicago, Illinois Press, 1998.

Laseau, Paul, and James Tice. *Frank Lloyd Wright: Between Principle and Form.* New York: Van Nostrand Reinhold, 1992.

Levine, Neil. *The Architecture of Frank Lloyd Wright.* Princeton, NJ: Princeton University Press, 1997.

Lind, Carla. *The Wright Style.* London: Thames and Hudson, 1992.

———. *Lost Wright: Frank Lloyd Wright's Vanished Masterpieces.* New York: Simon & Schuster, 1996.

———. *Frank Lloyd Wright's Life and Homes.* "Wright at a Glance" series. San Francisco: Pomegranate, 1994.

———. *Frank Lloyd Wright's First Houses.* Wright at a Glance. San Francisco: Pomegranate, 1996.

———. *Frank Lloyd Wright's Usonian Houses.* Wright at a Glance. San Francisco: Pomegranate, 1994.

———. *Frank Lloyd Wright's California Houses.* Wright at a Glance. San Francisco: Pomegranate, 1996.

———. *Frank Lloyd Wright's Fallingwater.* Wright at a Glance. San Francisco: Pomegranate, 1996.

———. *Frank Lloyd Wright's Public Buildings.* Wright at a Glance. San Francisco: Pomegranate, 1996.

———. *Frank Lloyd Wright's Glass Designs.* Wright at a Glance. San Francisco: Pomegranate, 1995.

———. *Frank Lloyd Wright's Fireplaces.* Wright at a Glance. San Francisco: Pomegranate, 1995.

———. *Frank Lloyd Wright's Dining Rooms.* Wright at a Glance. San Francisco: Pomegranate, 1995.

———. *Frank Lloyd Wright's Furnishings.* Wright at a Glance. San Francisco: Pomegranate, 1995.

———. *Frank Lloyd Wright's Lost Buildings.* Wright at a Glance. San Francisco: Pomegranate, 1994.

Maddex, Diane. *Fifty Favorite Rooms by Frank Lloyd Wright.* New York: Smithmark Publishers, 1998.

Manson, Grant. *The Early Work of Frank Lloyd Wright: The "Ausgefuhrte Bauten" of 1911.* New York: Dover, 1982.

McCarter, Robert. *Fallingwater: Frank Lloyd Wright.* London: Phaidon, 1994.

———. *Frank Lloyd Wright: A Primer on Architectural Principles.* New York: Princeton Architectural Press, 1991.

McDonough, Yona Zeldis. *Frank Lloyd Wright.* New York: Chelsea House, 1992.

Meehan, Patrick J. *Frank Lloyd Wright Remembered.* Washington, DC: National Trust for Historic Preservation, 1991.

———. *Truth Against the World: Frank Lloyd Wright Speaks for an Organic Architecture.* Washington, DC: The Preservation Press, 1992.

Moran, Maya. *Down To Earth: An Insider's View of Frank Lloyd Wright's Tomek House.* Carbondale, IL: Southern Illinois University Press, 1995.

Murphy, Wendy. *Frank Lloyd Wright.* Parsippany, NJ: Silver Burdett Press, 1990.

Nemtin, Frances. *Frank Lloyd Wright and Taliesin.* Rohnert Park, CA: Pomegranate, 2000.

Nute, Kevin. *Frank Lloyd Wright & Japan.* London: Chapman & Hall, 1993.

Patterson, Terry L. *Frank Lloyd Wright: The Meaning of Materials.* New York: Van Nostrand Reinhold, 1994.

Pfeiffer, Bruce Brooks. *Frank Lloyd Wright: The Masterworks.* New York: Rizzoli in association with the Frank Lloyd Wright Foundation, 1993.*

Quinan, Jack. *Frank Lloyd Wright's Larkin Building: Myth and Fact.* New York: Architectural History Foundation, MIT, 1987.

Rattenbury, John. *A Living Architecture.* Toronto: Warwick Publishing, 1999.

Scoular, David B. *The First Decade.* Tempe, AZ: Arizona State University, 1976.

Secrest, Meryle. *Frank Lloyd Wright: A Biography.* New York: HarperTrade, 1993.

Sergeant, John. *Frank Lloyd Wright's Usonian Houses: The Case for Organic Architecture.* New York: Whitney Library of Design, 1976.*

Simo, Melanie. *Barnsdall Park.* Washington: Spacemaker Press, 1995.

Smith, Kathryn. *Frank Lloyd Wright's Hollyhock House & Olive Hill.* New York: Rizzoli, 1992.

Sprague, Paul, ed. et al. *Frank Lloyd Wright & Madison: Eight Decades of Artistic and Social Interaction.* Madison, WI: University of Wisconsin and Elvejham Museum of Art, 1990.

Steele, James. *Barnsdall House: Frank Lloyd Wright.* London: Phaidon, 1992.

Tafel, Edgar. *Years with Frank Lloyd Wright: Apprentice to Genius.* New York: Dover, 1985.

———, ed. *About Wright: An Album of Recollections by Those who Knew Frank Lloyd Wright.* New York: John Wiley, 1993.

Thompson, Iain. *Frank Lloyd Wright: A Visual Encyclopedia.* San Diego: Thunder Bay Press, 1999.

Tiltman, Hessell. The Imperial Hotel Story. Tokyo: Privately printed, 1970.

Twombly, Robert C. *Frank Lloyd Wright, His Life and His Architecture.* New York: John Wiley, 1979.

Watterson, Kathryn. *Building a Dream: The Sarah Smith Story.* Santa Barbara, CA: Smith Publishing, 1999.

Storrer, William Allin. *The Architecture of FLLW: A Complete Catalogue.* Cambridge, MA: M.I.T. Press, 1978.

———. *A Frank Lloyd Wright Companion.* Chicago: University of Chicago Press, 1993.

ABOUT ARCHITECTURE, CONSTRUCTION, ENVIRONMENT, PHILOSOPHY, AND THE FUTURE

Alexander, Christopher, et al. *A Pattern Language: Towns, Buildings, Construction.* New York: Oxford University Press, 1977.

American Institute of Architects. *Architects Handbook of Energy Practice.* Washington, D.C.: AIA, 1982.

American Institute of Architects Research Corporation. *Solar Dwelling Design Concepts.* Washington, D.C.: U.S. Department of Housing and Urban Development (HUD), 1976.

Ander, Gregg. *Daylighting Performance and Design.* 2nd ed. New York: John Wiley, 2003.

Anderson, Bruce, and Malcolm Wells. *Passive Solar Energy.* Amherst, NH: Brick House Publishing, 1981.

Baggs, Sydney, and Joan Baggs. *The Healthy House.* New York: Harper Collins, 1996.*

Barrie, Thomas, and Gyorgy Doczi. *Spiritual Path, Sacred Place: Myth, Ritual and Meaning in Architecture.* Boston: Shambala, 1996.

Brown, Azby. *Small Spaces: Stylish Ideas for Making More of Less in the Home.* New York: Kodansha, 1996.

Butler, G. Montague. *Handbook of Mineralogy, Blowpipe Analysis and Geometrical Crystallography.* New York: John Wiley, c1918.

Callender, John Hancock, ed. *Time-Saver Standards: A Handbook of Architectural Design.* New York: McGraw-Hill, 1966.

Chiazzari, Suzy. *The Healing Home.* North Pomfret, VT: Trafalgar Square, 1998.*

Copestick, Joanna. *The Family Home.* New York: Stewart, Tabori & Chang, 1998.

Cutler, Laurence, and Sherrie Cutler. *Handbook of Housing Systems for Designers and Developers.* New York: Van Nostrand & Reinhold, 1974.

Egan, M. David. *Concepts in Thermal Comfort.* Paramus, NJ: Prentice-Hall, 1975.

Eisely, Loren. *The Immense Journey.* New York: Vintage Books, 1959.

Foerster, Bernd. *Pattern and Texture.* Washington, DC: Allied Masonry Council, 1961.

Goldwater, Barry. *The Coming Breakpoint.* New York: Macmillan Publishing, 1976.

Gracian, Baltasar. *The Art of Worldly Wisdom.* New York: Barnes and Noble, 1993.

Guthrie, Pat. *The Architect's Portable Handbook.* 2nd ed. New York: McGraw-Hill, 1998.

Harwood, Barbara B. *The Healing House: How Living in the Right House Can Heal You Spiritually, Emotionally, and Physically.* Carlsbad, CA: Hay House, 1997.

Hawken, Paul, Amory Lovins, and L. Hunter Lovins. *The Ecology of Commerce: A Declaration of Sustainability.* New York: HarperBusiness, 1993.

———, et al. *Natural Capitalism: Creating the Next Industrial Revolution.* New York: Little, Brown & Company, 2000.

Hawking, Stephen. *The Universe in a Nutshell.* New York: Bantam Books, 2001.

Hermannsson, John. *Green Building Resource Guide.* Newtown, CT: Taunton Press, 1997.

Hornbostel, Caleb, and William Hornung. *Materials & Methods for Contemporary Construction.* Englewood Cliffs, NJ: Prentice-Hall, 1982.

Housing Press. *The House & Home Kitchen Planning Guide.* New York: McGraw-Hill, 1978.

Jankowski, Wanda. *Designing with Light: Residential Interiors.* Glen Cove, NY: PBC International, 1992.

Johnson, Glenn M. *The Art of Illumination: Residential Lighting Design.* New York: McGraw-Hill, 1999.

Kemper, Alfred M. *Architectural Handbook: Environmental Analysis, Architectural Programming, Design and Technology, and Construction.* New York: Wiley, 1979.

Kunstler, James H. *The Geography of Nowhere: The Rise and Decline of America's Man-Made Landscape.* New York: Free Press, 1994.

———. *Home From Nowhere: Remaking our Everyday World for the 21st Century.* NY: Touchstone, 1998.

Lawlor, Anthony. *A Home for the Soul.* New York: Clarkson N. Potter, 1997.

Littlejohn, David, ed. *The Real Las Vegas: Life Beyond the Strip.* New York: Oxford University Press, 1999.

Lovelock, J. E. *Gaia: A New Look at Life on Earth.* Oxford: Oxford University Press, 1979.

Lovins, Amory B. et al. *Energy Unbound: A Fable for America's Future.* San Francisco: Sierra Club Books, 1987.

Moyers, Bill. *A World of Ideas.* New York: Doubleday, 1989.

Murray, Elizabeth. *Cultivating Sacred Space: Gardening for the Soul.* San Francisco: Pomegranate, 1997.

Naisbitt, John. *Megatrends: Ten New Directions Transforming Our Lives.* New York: Warner Books, 1984.

———, and Patricia Aburdene. *Megatrends 2000.* New York: William Morrow, 1990.

———. *Re-Inventing the Corporation: Transforming Your Job and Your Company for the New Information Society.* New York: Warner Books, 1985.

Nuckolls, James L. *Interior Lighting for Environmental Designers.* Hoboken, NJ: John Wiley, 1983.

Okakura, Kakuzo. *Book of Tea.* New York: Dover, 1964.

Papanek, Victor. *The Green Imperative: Ecology and Ethics in Design and Architecture.* London: Thames & Hudson, 1995.

Parker, Alfred Browning. *You and Architecture.* New York: Delacorte Press, 1965.

Pople, Nicolas. *Experimental Houses.* New York: Watson-Guptill Publications, 2000.

Preiser, Wolfgang F.E., ed., et al. *Universal Design Handbook.* New York: McGraw-Hill, 2001.

Ramsey, Charles and Harold Reeve Sleeper. *Architectural Graphic Standards for Architects, Engineers, Decorators, Builders and Draftsmen.* New York: John Wiley, 1951.

Rogers, Tyler Stewart. *Thermal Design of Buildings.* New York: John Wiley, 1964.

Santayana, George. *The Sense of Beauty.* New York: Dover, 1955.

Schram, Joseph F. *Modern Bathrooms.* Menlo Park, CA: Lane Book Company, 1963.

Stevens, Peter S. *Patterns in Nature.* New York: Little Brown & Co., 1974.

Storey, Sally. *Lighting: Simple Solutions for the Home.* San Francisco: Chronicle Books, 2000.

Strong, Steven J., with William G. Scheller. *The Solar Electric House.* Massachusetts: Sustainability Press, 1993.

Susanka, Sarah. *Creating the Not So Big House.* Newtown, CT: Taunton Press, 2001.

———. *The Not So Big House: A Blueprint for the Way We Really Live.* Newtown, CT: Taunton Press, 2001.*

Swaback, Vernon D. *Designing the Future.* Phoenix Dialogues Series, Vol. 1. Tempe, AZ: Herberger Center for Design Excellence, 1997.

Tucker, William. *Progress and Privilege: America in the Age of Environmentalism.* New York: Doubleday, 1982.

Walters, Derek. *Feng Shui: The Chinese Art of Designing a Harmonious Environment.* New York: Fireside, 1989.*

Wasowski, Andy, with Sally Wasowski. *Building Inside Nature's Envelope.* New York: Oxford University Press, 2000.*

Wright, David. *Natural Solar Architecture: A Passive Primer.* New York: Van Nostrand Reinhold, 1978.